To:

The Resi...

MCG + RL...

of

All The Best,

G.S...

'03

MCG&RC
Residents
Book Club

THOSE ARE THE BREAKS:

A COLLECTION OF MEMORIES

By
Gregory J. Smith

Copyright © 2003 by Gregory J. Smith

ISBN 0-7414-1558-5

E-mail-Gapsmith@aol.com

Published by:

PUBLISHING.COM

519 West Lancaster Avenue
Haverford, PA 19041-1413
Info@buybooksontheweb.com
www.buybooksontheweb.com
Toll-free (877) BUY BOOK
Local Phone (610) 520-2500
Fax (610) 519-0261

Printed in the United States of America

Printed on Recycled Paper

Published July 2003

DEDICATION

To my Mom, for her undying love and support. I love you!

SPECIAL THANKS

To Bill Lyon, from The Philadelphia Inquirer, for his guidance, encouragement and support regarding this project. Thanks also to my brother Mark, who guided me through the dreaded world of the word processor. Thanks for your patience and skill.

Extra special thanks to my wonderful family and friends, to Bobby Rydell, Bobby Wine and Barry Manilow; to all the doctors and nurses who helped me through out my life; to all the staff, residents and clients I worked with over the years; and to everyone (sorry if I forgot someone) who touched my life. This story is for you.

Final thanks to Dave Giorgio and everyone at Infinity Publishing for their kindness, support and assistance. Without you there would not be a book.

TABLE OF CONTENTS

CHAPTERS

FORWARD

Over the years many people have encouraged me to write my life story. I always resisted, never thinking my story was worth reading.

Recently a "little voice" inside told me to "do it". I always listen to that inner voice because it is usually correct. So I took a chance and started to write. I soon realized that I had no other choice, as if I didn't have a say in the matter.

I found very little information about my condition in my research, let alone first-person accounts. It gave me another challenge, another goal, another hill to overcome, just to see if I could do it.

This story is dedicated to anyone who has been labeled as "different". It is for the physically, mentally, and emotionally challenged, and for anyone in need, who is looking for some hope and inspiration. It is especially devoted to those few of us who have Osteogenisis Imperfecta, or families and loved ones close to someone afflicted with O.I. My wish and prayer for you is that in some small way, my story will offer encouragement to overcome any adversity and be the best you can be. Please, don't ever give up!

My story is also intended for the able-bodied as well. Perhaps in some small way, it will break down barriers, misconceptions, and allow you to see that we are one, not so "different" after all.

1. IT'S A LONG WAY UP

I have Osteogenisis Imperfecta. Brittle bone disease. I had literally hundreds of fractures as a kid. So many, in fact, they eventually lost count.

I mention my physical challenge from the start, because O.I. has been the centerpiece of my life. Almost everything in my life revolved around my condition.

My Mom and I often pondered. what my life would have been like if I didn't have O.I. How would I have turned out/ Still a good guy, or maybe a drug dealer? Fate and destiny are funny that way. Everything seems to fall into place, as you will see as my story unfolds.

Even I don't know much about my condition. I have tried researching O.I. on the Internet, but there really isn't that much information out there, the condition is so rare. What I have found out is, it's a genetic disorder, often on the mothers' side; one out of several million people has it, usually the life expectancy is about 25 years; and, there is no cure.

Even though O.I is classified as a genetic disorder, Mom claimed I was perfectly normal and even walked, up until my first fall. Who knows? I may have been born with fractures as so many O.I babies are, but it just never manifested itself until one night when I was 21 months old.

I would rather not think about the possibility that I already had broken bones when I was born at 6:15 am on Friday, November 16, 1956.

Mom named me Gregory after St. Gregory the Great. His feast day was November 17. My parents weren't sure of a name, so they went with Gregory. If I was a girl I would have been named Gertrude (since St. Gertrude's feast day is November 16).

Gerty? I'm glad I turned out to be a guy.

It's a terrible thought, having fractures in the womb, being slapped by the doctor, crying, with the doctors and nurses thinking it was a healthy cry, not a cry from pain. What a way to enter the world!

It was bath night. I loved going into my room as the tub filled with bubbling water, getting a dry wash cloth out of the drawer, then tossing it into the water with a splash, and watching it sink to the bottom.

Giggling, my cute dimples showed even then. Little things like that made me happy.

As fate would have it, on this night the linoleum in my bedroom was wet. I slipped on my way to the drawer, fell and broke the femur bone in my left leg.

That single moment was the start of a new life. They rushed me to the local hospital, where they put my leg in traction. Now, I don't know if this was common practice with little kids back in the late 1950s, instead of casting the leg, but that is the treatment they gave me.

During my stay in the hospital someone moved the traction. Never found out whom. A nurse? A cleaning lady? A family member by accident?

My left leg started to swell, my toes turning blue. Poor circulation- but why? They couldn't figure it out.

So they transferred me down to one of the big city hospitals- the old Children's Hospital in nearby Philadelphia, Pennsylvania. That was my first encounter with the famous Dr. Nicholson. It wouldn't be my last.

Dr. Nicholson was a world-renowned bone specialist. He was the best, and he would be my savior as a child. We had a lot of tough times together and seeing him always meant pain and suffering, but he had such a cool, calming effect on me, and I trusted him so much. Not that I ever looked forward to seeing him.

He was tall and thin, razor-sharp blue eyes behind round wire-rimmed glasses, with short snowy white hair and a British accent that made him sound very cool and distinguished. I would think of him as the perfect Dr. Livingstone in the jungles of Africa, with a friendly Marcus Welby quality about him.

For some strange reason he always called me "Jeffrey", but I never knew why. His final parting line was always, "See you, until you need me again."

Who knew, at that first meeting, how much I would need him back then?

Once Nicholson saw the condition of my leg, first, he was mad- why wait so long to transfer me? He whisked me into the operating room without delay. I think of my poor parents and what they had to be going through. Their fourth son, not even two years old, rushed into the OR Would they ever see me again?

Upon opening my leg Nicholson found the problem-the bone was not knitting properly. All the marrow and calcium were leaking underneath the tissue. That is why the leg was growing to several times its normal size.

After the surgery, over a cup of coffee, Nicholson told my parents of the events in the operating room. How he had to step away from the table- the odor from the leaking marrow was so bad. How he had to make a decision right there, a quick decision but one, which would affect my entire life.

Amputate the leg or save it?

He saved the leg, cleaned it out, but I had lost too much calcium. After that, no matter how much calcium they shot into me, it was never enough.

And so began the vicious cycle of fracturing a bone, wearing a plaster cast for six to eight weeks, then fracturing again. In and out of hospitals. Ambulance trips, anytime, day or night. From school, from church, from home.

I broke all my limbs and my back in every way imaginable- sneezing or coughing too hard, turning over, awake or in my sleep, even once merely tossing a beanbag during a game.

Snap! I would break. The doctors started calling me "China Baby" because my bones shattered like glass. I still remember feeling each break, but hearing it as well, the terrible crunch of bones breaking.

For a little kid, I didn't know what to think. I should have been more worried about collecting baseball cards or comic books- not about my next fracture.

That's the thing about O.I.- not only does it hurt each time a fracture occurs (although during the years my tolerance for pain grew)- but it's also very painful psychologically. I was always thinking of the next fracture, afraid not to move or twist so quickly, always with a certain degree of anxiety and caution constantly on my mind.

It never went away. A terrible way to feel.

But thankfully, I was young enough so I really didn't know any better. To me, being in and out of a cast every few months was normal. Not being able to do things other kids could do was normal. There was no other way. What else could I do but accept my life?

Pretty soon, the words Osteogenisis Imperfecta were burned into my brain. It was marked everywhere-on charts, x-rays. I would even tell interns or nurses what my condition was before they asked.

"Oh, I have Osteogenisis Imperfecta." No big deal.

I didn't know it was very rare. I also didn't know that the doctors were telling my parents I probably wouldn't live long. They thought the stress of the constant fractures would eventually take its toll on my frail body. If I lived past the age of sixteen, when my bones would get stronger and my body would mature, well, maybe I would make it.

But that was a long way to go.

Although I endured many fractures over the years, several stand out in my mind. Even to this day I still remember them and can feel them.

The Back-Breaker- Remember the old saying, "Step on a crack, break your Mother's. back"? Well, this time it was my back.

My older brother was simply pushing me in a coach down the street. We were getting ready to go to our towns' annual Dogwood Parade .It was mid-May, a warm, sunny spring day.

We went over a crack in the sidewalk and crunch! Two vertebrae in my back were crushed.

I'll never forget the terrible pain, so different then my previous leg fractures. I couldn't sit down or lie down. Instead of going to the parade that day I had an unexpected appointment with another ambulance ride. And Dr. Nicholson again.

Maybe the worst part of this incident was that I had to wear a full body cast for several months. Only my arms and head were free to move. I couldn't do anything for myself, and even had trouble eating since I was stuck in the prone position.

After the body cast was removed I wore a corset for a long time. A constant reminder of that single fracture.

The Three-Limb Fracture- My Dad was carrying me home from church one Sunday morning (he used to carry me everywhere back then, like Tiny Tim, maybe because I was small. I didn't get into the wheelchair phase yet). He slipped on a patch of ice, and fell. Luckily, Dad wasn't hurt- but I broke both my legs and shattered my elbow.

I never saw him so upset, blaming himself, but it wasn't his fault. It just happened. I tried not to cry, waiting for the ambulance, and begged him not to feel bad.

I could deal with the leg fractures. The shattered elbow was the real pain. Since it was totally broken into pieces they had to surgical repair it. They casted it first, put it in traction but didn't operate right away. Dr. Nicholson was away for a few days and they decided to wait until his return later in the week. Until then spasms shot through my arm every few seconds, and they tried to control the pain with medicine.

I was never so glad to see Nicholson in my life. We had sort of a love/hate relationship. I loved him for his help, and trusted him immensely. But I also dreaded seeing him each time, as I knew he symbolized pain.

The Birthday Break- it was a happy day, not only because it was my seventh birthday, but I was also getting another cast off. And we were having spaghetti for dinner, my favorite.

But right before dinner I slipped on a rug and down I went. Not just a bruise or bump like an ordinary kid would have from a fall. Another fracture. Another ride to the hospital. Another cast.

So much for the spaghetti, but when I got home I still had enough energy to blow out the candles on my birthday cake.

Soon I grew very familiar with Children's Hospital. It was like my second home. The old, gray stone building looked like a cold English castle from the outside- or a mausoleum- depending on your outlook.

The room I dreaded the most was the infamous Cast Room. It was a small room on the first floor, painted all in white. The scent of plaster hung in the air. This was the place where they applied and removed all the casts. The room of broken bones. Different sizes of electric saws hung on the walls. Like a modern day torture chamber.

I hated saws. The sound of them, the warmth when they buzzed close to the skin. Then after Nicholson split the cast in two, he would pry apart the plaster with a giant pair of tongs.

There was the leg, wrapped around cotton and gauze, as weak and fragile as a newborn chick just hatched from an egg. I used to look at the sight, and not even think it was my leg, like it was detached from my body. From then on it was a regular routine of rehabilitation-until the next break.

I also hated casts, especially in the summer, when they were so hot to wear. But I got pretty good at scratching an itch with a pencil or ruler, even though Nicholson always warned me against this tactic.

More importantly then the building itself, I grew familiar with the people within- nurses, orderlies, and the other patients. They knew me too, since I was there so often, and would greet me and my parents with "Back again?"

There were so many people. Names came and went. Sometimes I met people who were nameless, yet always remained in my memory.

Like the cute nurse from the Philippines, who cheered me up one time during a hospital stay, by singing "You Are My Sunshine" with me. I'll never forget it, that she took the time to make me smile or the cheerful orderly, who cracked jokes and made me laugh on my way to surgery one morning. Mom wasn't there; I was scared, lonely, crying. He somehow made me laugh on the elevator, on the way up to the OR. Again, I never got a name, or don't remember it, but I never forgot the kindness.

One special friend I'll always remember from my hospital stays was Michelle. She seemed to be in the hospital almost as much as I was. She was a pretty girl, a few years older then I, maybe in her early teens. She had long brown hair, nice legs and a great smile. She loved Davy Jones and The Monkees, who were popular at the time. We often talked, and her room was close to mine. We became friends and consoled each other through the tough, lonely times, and complained to each other about the food and the pain.

I never really fully understood why Michelle was in the hospital. All I heard was the word "Leukemia" but I didn't know what it meant. I think my parents and even Michelle didn't want to tell me much.

One time when I went back to the hospital, either for a check-up or to have a cast removed, we met Michelle's Mom at the elevator. We thought Michelle was back in the hospital again, and thought we would stop by to see her while we were there.

Michelle's Mom informed us that Michelle had died the night before. She was there to pick up her clothes and personal items. But she wanted me to have something special from Michelle. She had no idea I was going to be there. It was a picture of Michelle, a school photo, and it simply said on the back "With love, Michelle'.

I still have that picture and think of her fondly.

Did I ever get depressed, being around pain and death and suffering and sadness all the time? Sure, who wouldn't? But more then sadness, loneliness was my biggest issue. I never asked "Why me?" Again, I thought my life was normal.

If it weren't for the tremendous support of family and friends, I never would have survived those early years.

Dad was a great guy. He was my hero. He grew up in an orphanage. He was a World War II vet, fighting in the Battle of the Bulge in Europe, then worked as a machinist at a local tire factory for over 30 years, often working overtime and weekends just to make ends meet. My parents literally went from paycheck to paycheck. I'm sure my medical expenses didn't help.

6

Dad was an avid bowler, and when my health permitted, he took me up to the local bowling alley every Sunday to watch his league games, and even to keep score now and then. Those were exciting times, watching my Dads' team (he was Captain), Sacred Heart White. Most were made up of our family members In fact, at one point the team consisted of Dad, my Uncle Franny (who averaged close to 180), and my brothers Jimmy, Pat and Tommy. They never won the championship, always the underdogs, but it gave me something to look forward to each Sunday night.

Dad loved Baseball too, as I did, and we went to as many games as we could. Later, I'll relate our first game together in person, and after that; we would always look forward to baseball season, picking out our games to attend each year. We couldn't wait to get the schedule for the following season. I remember the thrill of getting the tickets in the mail, or even going down to the stadium in late winter to buy tickets for the upcoming summer. Again, it gave us both something to look forward to.

The stress had to be incredible for my folks. When I think about it now, I don't know how they did it. I guess you have to deal with the cards you are dealt in life, and their love and perseverance rubbed off on me later in life. I was fighting my illness, but they were fighters too.

Mom was always by my side. The Rock of the family. A former practical nurse, she quit her job to take care of me when my O.I. developed. Often she would spend the night in the hospital with me. Or she would drive the Schuylkill Expressway -about an hour drive, to see me each day, sometimes with Dad or without. He had to work, and someone had to stay with my brothers and sisters.

Mom always brought me a toy when I was in the hospital. Often she would walk around the corner of the hospital to a local store, and one time a cop stopped her and warned her about the unsafe neighborhood. He walked her to the store and back again.

At home, she bathed me, fed me. Helped with my bathroom duties, often the baths were sponge baths, since I was in a cast most of the time I couldn't get into a shower or tub. Mom stayed by my bedside many hours, holding my hand, praying, keeping me company.

I just can't say enough about her. She was very religious, and always believed a miracle would occur, and I would be OK. We all had a pretty strong faith in God, but hers was the strongest. I never knew of anyone with so much faith.

Otherwise she was a typical mom. Maybe a little over-protective at times, but what mom isn't? She was a great cook, always sent get-well cards to people who were sick; she was always doing something for someone in need. A sweet woman.

Those nights in the hospital I would hear other kids cry, either out of pain or loneliness, wanting to go home. It was heartbreaking. The next morning I would keep my eyes peeled down the hall, and when I saw mom emerge from the elevator I would yell out loud, "Here comes my Mommy!"

I gave my parents a lot of credit. They could have easily "put me away" into an institution, not deal with it. But they never gave up on me, and wouldn't allow me to give up on myself. That life lesson would follow me forever. Whenever I would come across troubled waters down the road, I remembered my parents' love and devotion. They were my bridges over those waters, the inspiration I often needed to continue on.

My brothers and sisters were great too. I had 4 brothers, Jimmy, Tommy, Pat, Mark and 1 sister (the poor thing), Phyllis. I can imagine it was tough on them too, the chaos which at any moment could disrupt their lives. A lot of times my parents were with me at the hospital, so the other kids got used to fending for themselves, making dinner, cleaning the house. Many times they kept me company at home, reading to me or playing a game, when they could have been out with their friends. But they always supported me, no matter what, and for that I loved them dearly.

I thought it might be tough on them, the stigma of having a sibling whom was "different". What would their friends say? But they always tried to involve me in their lives and make my life as normal as possible, even if it just meant a game of wiffle ball in the backyard.

Friends were a big part of my early life. Visitors brightened my spirits. Get well cards were appreciated and hung on the bulletin board near my bed. Many people prayed for me, and I really believe their thoughts, prayers and visits helped to get me through some of those dark times.

It would be impossible to mention or thank everyone involved in my early childhood. But there was one special person who touched me a great deal in those years.

Her name was Monica and she lived around the block. She went to the same church as we did, so her family knew mine. She again was older (what was it with older women and me?); She would stop by after school and always bring me a bag of candy from the local store. She made me cards, and we often colored on my bedroom floor or read books together. She baby-sat for me at times too.

The days she didn't stop by, I would look out our front window and miss her. Once, during a snowstorm, I watched her across the street, having a snowball fight with her friends. I wished I could be one of her "normal" friends too, but I guess I was a special friend to her. It was good to have a friend like Moni, who cared.

The things she bought me- the candy, the toys, and the cards- she bought out of her own allowance. I didn't appreciate her sweetness and kindness until later in life, and she was a big inspiration to me, a shining example that I would try to copy later in my life as a social worker.

I guess I had a crush on Moni. She was older and pretty. When she started dating guys and visiting less, I was jealous and my heart ached. When she eventually got married I was happy for her, but cried on her wedding day. Realistically, I knew it could never be, although fairy tale romances would appear in my life later. That was hard, crushes, most of them one-way crushes. She ended up having several kids, and became a nurse, again helping the sick and others in need. Ironically, we would work at the same nursing home years later, side by side.

Having an illness did have some advantages. My early life wasn't all sadness and pain. I had a lot of happy times too. Several special things kept me going.

Word got around about my condition and Dad arranged for me to meet two of my childhood idols- singer Bobby Rydell and Phillies shortstop Bobby Wine.

Bobby Rydell was a popular singer from nearby South Philadelphia. He was a teen idol back in the late fifties and early sixties. I remember at four years old watching Bobby on American Bandstand, my coal black hair slicked back in a pompadour like his, collecting all of his records, singing along to his songs. I spent hours, listening to his music on the old record player.

I always wanted to be a singer, and I even had my first gig at the tender age of four. I remember Mom hauling the portable record player to the local convent so that I could perform all of my Bobby Rydell hits before the nuns. I even had the body gestures down pat. The good sisters got a big kick out of it. I was too young to know any better.

Then Dad arranged for me to meet Bobby at the old Steel Pier in Atlantic City, New Jersey, where he was performing. I remember sitting on Bobby's lap, singing "Volaire" with him in his dressing room before the show. I kept the many autographed photos and his personalized scrapbook he gave me. Whenever I needed a boost of cheer, I would page through the scrapbook, which Bobby's mother had made for him. Imagine he gave it to me! I kept it up to date with loving care.

He was a great guy. During the show, he dedicated "our" song, "Volaire' to me as I watched from the audience, among several hundred screaming young girls. We said goodbye in the dressing room after the show but he would continue to be in my life, even years later.

Several months after we met, he wrote me a letter, commenting how sharp I looked that day, in my sporty blazer and bow tie. Most of all, he wrote near the end of the letter, that if he ever had a little brother, he wished he could be just like me.

Thirty years later we met again, in Atlantic City, but this time at Caesars after a show. Dad had been gone over ten years. Mom was there, and so was Phyllis. Bobby was nice enough to come out to the arena after the show, when I told the usher I had met him thirty years earlier, and wondered if I could just say hello.

I took the scrapbook with me and we reminisced about the good times. Bobby had his own kids now, and even grandchildren, and although I cherished the book, I gave the scrapbook back to Bobby, not because I didn't want it or love it anymore, but that he could share the memories with his family now. He was touched by this gesture. . It was good to know that we had both made it, after so many years.

Baseball was a real passion of mine. I loved all sports, but Baseball was number one. My favorite team was the Philadelphia Phillies. They didn't win very often back in the sixties, but they were still my team. I kind of identified with the Phils- they were scrappy, never gave up and were fighters too.

I used to watch all the games on TV. I listened to the games on the radio, which weren't on the tube, even the West Coast late night games, with my little transistor radio tucked under my pillow at night. If I fell asleep before the game ended, Dad would always leave a note by my bed in the morning before he went to work, giving me the news if the Phils won or lost, and the score.

I collected Baseball cards, like most kids did. Nothing like the bubble gum aroma of a pack of new Baseball cards. It was always a thrill to open the pack and find out what players you got to complete your checklist. Then, of course, you would trade your doubles with other kids in the neighborhood, or flip cards. I was a pretty good flipper in my time, and won extra cards, which I needed for my collection.

My favorite player back then was Phils shortstop Bobby Wine. He couldn't hit a lick, but he was probably the best defensive shortstop of his time. He possessed a rocket arm and his glove gobbled up ground balls like a vacuum cleaner. I loved his style and ease when playing the field. And maybe because he couldn't hit, he was again my underdog.

Well, my Dad knew someone from work that was a neighbor of Bobby Wine. So as a surprise on my birthday, Dad arranged for Bobby to call me, which he did, wishing me a Happy Birthday. I was in heaven.

especially when he asked me to come to a game the following season.

"Hurry up and get better," he said, "because I want to see you at a game next year".

That alone gave me enough incentive to not give up hope.

The following season my dream came true. I had never actually been to a Major League Baseball game before. So when Dad bought the tickets I was thrilled. I just prayed nothing would happen to mess it up, like a fracture. I had fractured the morning of an Eagles/Vikings football game, also the first football game I was planning to attend. Needless to say, there was no football for me that Sunday afternoon.

But God and good fortune were on my side, as I stayed healthy enough to go to the game. My beloved Phillies were playing the dreaded Los Angeles Dodgers that Sunday, a hot ticket, as the Dodgers had a great team, with the likes of Sandy Koufax and Don Drysdale on their team. David versus Goliath, but I didn't care. I hoped the Phils would win, as always, but I was just happy to attend a game in person.

My heart pounded as we approached old Connie Mack Stadium in Philadelphia. Usually the only time I saw Philly was for a hospital visit, so it was nice to be in the city for a much happier occasion. I saw the light towers in the distance as we drove closer to the stadium, and it felt like a dream, a dream I experienced many times before. But this was real!

Dad carried me as we walked up to the stadium gates. I peered inside and could see the parrot green grass of the outfield. I could smell the hot dogs, the peanuts, and the onions. The buzz of the crowd thrilled me, the yells of "Get 'Yer Program Here!" from the vendor.

When we got inside the stadium I couldn't believe my eyes. To my surprise we descended down the aisle. And kept going and going. - until we reached the field level. My Dad had somehow got box seats for us. Right next to the Phillies dugout.

Everything was in front of me-the players, the grandstand, and the field. And everything was in color! Remember, back in those days, most televisions were still black and white, as mine was. Just the hugeness of the spectacle, and the vibrant colors amazed me. The blue in the Dodger uniform was so blue the red in the Phillies' caps as though I had been color blind before, and now was able to see.

I watched the players in front of me, and Koufax and Drydale right there, close enough to touch. Some of the Dodger pitchers were walking to the bullpen before the game started and they passed right by me. This was all enough-I would've been happy to go home then and there. But what happened next was something I would remember for a lifetime.

11

companionship. But we also had our share of cats, rabbits, turtles, fish, a mynah bird and even a duck (which would follow Mom around the yard as she hung laundry, and would quack at the front door when someone knocked).

Animals provided much laughter and fun. I still have a dog; a cute Pekinese puppy named Louie, who is my buddy, no matter what. Laughter is truly the best medicine. I really believed I felt better both physically and emotionally-with laughter and smiling in my life.

My family and friends tried to keep my life as "normal" as possible. We went on a family vacation one summer to visit my Uncle Steve in Los Angeles. We visited Disneyland while there, which was every little kid's fantasy come true. It was a three-week trip, as we loaded up the station wagon and drove cross-country and back again. We were just like the Griswalds in the "Family Vacation" movies. It was fun, and another thing to look forward to.

Other things in my life made me happy-spaghetti dinners every Sunday; holidays, especially Christmas and Easter, when the entire family got together and celebrated; simple times like watching TV with Dad on the living room floor, and laughing so hard at old Jerry Lewis movies or sitcoms like "The Honeymooners" or "All In The Family".

These simple, yet important events in my young life kept me going, and most importantly, made me smile. Positive moments in my life, to even out those times of pain. With life so precious during those early years, I appreciated the laughter and the fun even more. Later in life, with time to reflect, I cherished them even more, and realized just how special my family and friends really were- and continued to be.

physically and emotionally-with laughter and smiling in my life.

My family and friends tried to keep my life as "normal" as possible. We went on a family vacation one summer to visit my Uncle Steve in Los Angeles. We visited Disneyland while there, which was every little kid's fantasy come true. It was a three-week trip, as we loaded up the station wagon and drove cross-country and back again. We were just like the Griswalds in the "Family Vacation" movies. It was fun, and another thing to look forward to.

Other things in my life made me happy-spaghetti dinners every Sunday; holidays, especially Christmas and Easter, when the entire family got together and celebrated; simple times like watching TV with Dad on the living room floor, and laughing so hard at old Jerry Lewis movies or sitcoms like "The Honeymooners" or "All In The Family".

These simple, yet important events in my young life kept me going, and most importantly, made me smile. Positive moments in my life, to even out those times of pain. With life so precious during those early years, I appreciated the laughter and the fun even more. Later in life, with time to reflect, I cherished them even more, and realized just how special my family and friends really were- and continued to be.

Me- Standing!
Age 2

My first Communion
1964

With family
Tom, Phyllis, Pat, & Dad

Me in a body cast- age 3
with brothers Pat & Tommy

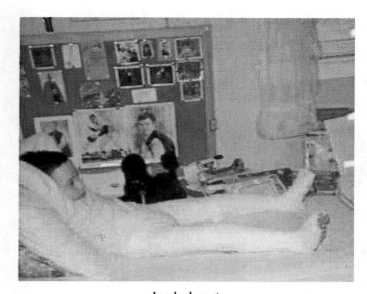

In a body cast
In my bedroom – age 12
Notice my "Bulletin Board of Hope" in the background

In Disneyland - 1969
with Pat, Dad, & Mark

BEAMING GREGORY Smith and his parents were guests of Greg's favorite,
Bobby Rydell, at Steel Pier in Atlantic City.

Bobby Rydell Brings Greg a 'Real Dream'

For' Gregory Smith, 4 1/2, it was a dream that came true when he
met his favorite recording star in a private audience at the Steel Pier in
Atlantic City recently. What other fellow his age could boast that he sat,
talked and sang with the teenager idol, Bobby Rydell, backstage before
and after the show?

The events leading up to this point create a pleasant story of nice people and how they react to offer a helping hand to less fortunates, especially little children.

Greg is the youngest child of Jim Smith from the Maintenance department and he is afflicted with a bone condition which has made him susceptible to fractures since he was 20 months old. He has been in and out of casts about nine times. This condition will persist until he reaches his teens. During these long periods of convalescing he became an avid viewer of American- Bandstand, the TV record and dance show. Here he saw and heard Bobby Rydell, a local Philadelphia boy, perform, and he became Greg's hero. The little fellow mimicked his voice and style, collected his records and developed one big desire to meet his favorite in person.

His father saw an advertisement announcing that Rydell was making a personal appearance at Steel Pier in Atlantic City, so he wrote to the management asking if it were possible to `arrange a meeting so his son 'could say hello or even shake hands with his favorite. A telegram arrived from Mr. Harnid, the owner of the pier, advising Jim to bring Greg to the shore and report to the pier box office.

When Jim, his wife and Greg presented themselves at the 'box office, they were ushered into the pier manager's office., After introductions, they went directly to Rydell's dressing room. What more could a fellow ask for - and Greg enjoyed every minute of the time, sitting on Rydell's lap, chatting and singing a duet to "Volaire," Rydell's hit record. Greg' received a personal scrapbook from his hero and was invited to be the special guest of the singer at his next performance. It was a front row seat for Greg, and a personal dedication of "their song" from the performer to his little friend.

After the show, the family returned again to the star's room and renewed acquaintances for another half hour. Greg went home literally on "Cloud Nine," about the most complete day a fellow of 4 1/2 can have. As his father put it, "There are no words to explain how we feel about this fine young boy and the other people involved who took time out to help him."

It goes to show — there are still nice people left in the world.

2. IT'S A MIRACLE

I made my First Communion the day before my 8th birthday, November 15, 1964. This was a memorable event, not only because it was my First Communion, but everything else that went with it.

There was a special 11:00 Mass that Sunday morning. I was dressed in a white suit, looking like an angel (or more like an early John Travolta). I remember the family threw a party in my honor, and I saw relatives and friends I didn't normally see who arrived from distances.

Again, it was a celebration, not only for the special day, but that I had lived until then, and also insurance, in case my condition became worse. My parents, God bless them, wanted me to have a memorable day- and a day, which they would never forget as well.

To mark the occasion, they asked a local photographer to take my picture after church, as I was still all dressed up. A lasting memory. Later, they would have that photo made into a portrait, and a local artist painted my picture from the photograph.

It still hangs on my bedroom wall, dimples flashing even then. It was kind of strange; having one's own portrait hovering over them, like I was already dead, but I realized the picture was more for my parents. Now, I can appreciate it more, and looking at it brings back memories and reminds me just how much my parents loved me, how much they sacrificed for me, and truthfully, how much they were afraid that my life would be a short one.

When it was time to enter school I spent the first eight years of my education in a special school for disabled kids in Norristown, PA. Back in the sixties they didn't integrate the physically challenged with so called: "normal" students. So I attended a school which was accessible-, all ramps, all on one floor. Most buildings back then were not accessible, with stairs a major obstacle to overcome. Steps were like mountains to me. This was way before the Americans with Disabilities act was passed, which lawfully made new buildings accessible and older buildings at least try to become accessible But now, we are still back in the Dark Ages.

I rode to school each day by taxicab with about four other disabled kids in the Phoenixville area. There was Denny, Timmy, Donny and Sy. All became close friends, maybe our only friends, baring in mind our similar situations. A nice guy named Joe drove us almost every day, and kept us smiling with jokes. I admired this fellow so much-he was like a grandfather to me- that when I made my confirmation I picked the name Joseph in his honor.

The students had different disabilities. Our cab rides would be noisy trips, full of stories and laughter. We had the same classes and tried to do the same recreational activities as anyone else. We had our normal fights but we never teased each other about our individual disability, probably because we knew we were all in the same boat.

There were certain aspects of grade school which stand out. My crush (yes, another crush) on my second- grade teacher. She was a pretty redhead, and I secretly fell for her. Then I found out, to my horror, not only was she married (so that's what the ring on her left hand meant!) but she was pregnant too.

I remember taking part in a Christmas play and having to sing. I was always a good singer, going back to my duet with Bobby Rydell, and a ham, going back to my singing with the nuns, so even though I was shy, I managed to pull it off with success.

I remember breaking a leg at school too. I was using a rolling walker back then, one with a seat and I had protection all around me. So I could still walk, which Nicholson encouraged, to build up the strength in my legs, but I could sit down too when I was tired. My parents and teachers would lift me out of the walker, as I took the walker home with me too.

I used to travel everywhere at 100 MPH, even later in life when I started using a wheelchair. One time I was flying down the halls at school and forgot to stop, slamming into a concrete wall. Just another break.

I did well in school but hated Math, an old annoyance that would haunt me later in life. As with the kids I met in the hospital I became more comfortable around issues like sickness, infirmity and even death. A classmate would suddenly die. There would be flowers on his or her desk the next day. We would accept this as a part of life and go on.

It sure made us grow up a lot faster.

During my Junior High days teachers came to my house after regular school hours. I was still fracturing as a teen, too fragile to attend school, plus the school itself was not accessible.

It was cool only having class one hour a day but I missed being with other kids, having friends to share lunch with, do homework, or just talk to. I started to become more socially isolated, a cocoon I would eventually break out of down the road. But for now, I missed being in the special school after so long.

Still, I continued to do well in my lessons, which amazed even me. There was always a misconception, which I noticed through out my life. If one is physically challenged society naturally feels one is either 1- paralyzed, despite your disability or 2- mentally challenged as well. I never could figure that out. I suppose it was ignorance, but often it was strange, when able-bodied people would raise their voice to me, or patronize me, thinking I couldn't understand them any other way. So I was glad I was doing well in school, showing society that if my body wasn't perfect at least my brain was functioning.

Jumping ahead a little, my High School days were still spent at home, only now I had an intercom system hooked up from my bedroom to school.

I affectionately became known as "The Box" for three years. Different students would unplug me and carry me from class to class. At times I spent class on the windowsill or in some classes I even had my own desk.

This was great because I could interact with the teachers and students by merely pressing a button. I still missed being with the kids, and I missed things like proms, but would try to make the football games in the fall. I spent most of my Friday and Saturday nights alone, knowing my peers were out having fun. And as I was maturing as a person I missed not having a girlfriend. Still had those innocent crushes, though.

Some of the kids would stop over my house after school and tutor me or bring homework. It was great putting a voice to a face. I guess they were just as curious about me, at least visiting once to see who this voice was in The Box. I couldn't see the blackboard, so subjects like Geometry were tough. Most of the teachers were kind and understanding, although a few were distant and cold. I guess they felt uncomfortable with this unique situation and didn't know how to handle the interaction and basic things like giving tests. Maybe some felt I was a needless burden in their world, an annoyance that they really didn't need.

It would have been easy to cheat. And some days I even had classes in my pajamas. But for the most part, it was as close to actually attending school as I could get, and again, I did fairly well in my studies.

The one day I actually attended school was for graduation on the football field. I met many of the voices in person that I grew so familiar with. After graduation everyone went his or her separate ways. I was left wondering what I wanted to do with my life, a subject I will touch upon later. But at least for that day I stood...or sat proudly. I graduated with honors despite Math, and even received a standing ovation when they gave out my diploma. One goal down and many more to go.

It was my parents' dream to take me to Lourdes.

The doctors continued to tell my brave parents that I might die due to the O.I. No one really knew for sure, because the condition was so rare. They felt if I lived past age sixteen I would have a chance to survive and lead a fairly normal life.

So when I was age fifteen we visited Lourdes, the famous Catholic shrine in southern France. The place for miracles. It was where Our Lady appeared eighteen times to a poor young peasant girl named Bernadette in 1858. My parents scraped together enough money to make the trip, borrowing, saving, and scrimping. Along with my youngest brother Mark we embarked on our own pilgrimage in August 1972.

During the apparitions, Our Lady of Lourdes had called for "penance". Indeed, as soon as we arrived our own personal penance began. The travel was hard. From Paris we transferred on to Lourdes. The airport was small, and I'll always remember my Dad carrying me down the stairs of the plane to a waiting wheelchair.

We were not on an organized pilgrimage. We were on our own for three weeks. We couldn't speak French. Looking back, I guess we were pretty brave.

I recall thinking that entering the shrine grounds was like entering Heaven itself. So quiet and peaceful, a world of difference considering the commercialism just outside the sanctuary gates, where souvenirs of all kinds were sold.

It was hard to believe we were really there, after such a long flight. Here was Lourdes-the majestic basilicas, the miraculous fountain, the Grotto itself, where hundreds of crutches hung, testaments of miracles through faith and prayer, the location were the Blessed Mother appeared.

A beautiful statue of Our Lady stood in the niche of the rock where she had graced her presence.

Needless to say, it was a humbling experience. But still I wasn't sure a kid my age could take in the importance of being there, and appreciate the sacrifice my parents made for me, especially Mom, who devotedly was convinced a miracle would occur.

I wondered if my faith was strong enough. Who was I to ask for a miracle? If it was God's will that I walk, why travel so far? Couldn't I be cured at home? I prayed to Mary to help me find an answer.

During our time in Lourdes we prayed many hours, both at the Grotto and in the numerous churches. Masses were said at all times; people of all nationalities knelt in constant prayer. Some sat on benches at the Grotto, saying the Rosary out loud, others prayers to themselves or in pilgrimage groups. Others just merely meditated. And the scene continued endlessly- no matter the hour, no matter the weather conditions.

We also visited St. Bernadette's home, where she had lived during the time of the apparitions. Actually, it was more a hovel then a house. It had formerly been a prison cell, and it's poverty left a lasting impression on me.

During our stay we met many inspirational people. One was a distinguished gray-haired sweet lady name Mrs. Feeley, who worked in the Lourdes Medical Building. She had been cured of cancer at Lourdes years ago. The bureau was the place where the miraculous cures were reported and verified.

During her daily lecture on the miracles of Lourdes, Mrs. Feeley provided impressive evidence of physical cures with photos and documents. She also talked about the many more spiritual healings, which occur each day. I'll never forget her story of how royalty from all over the world volunteer their time annually at Lourdes, working in the hospital or as stretcher-bearers, and doing so anonymously.

It was at one of these seminars where we met Brother Collins. This elderly Irish priest came to Lourdes each summer with a group of blind boys from a school in Dublin. Meeting his teenagers affected me greatly. Why would God allow innocent kids to be so afflicted?

As I shook each hand, I felt so sorry for them. Yet, they asked for no pity. Cheerful and quite normal, actually, they seemed to accept their situations. In fact, they weren't seeking miracles; rather, they returned each summer to be renewed in faith and hope, and to thank Our Lady and God for the blessings in their lives.

Suddenly, I didn't feel so helpless. If these young boys could make the best of their physically challenge, with faith and love, why couldn't I?

Since Our Lady had asked everyone to come to her in procession, at 4:30 each day there was a Blessing of the Sick in Rosary Square. I was fortunate enough to be involved in a number of these special blessings, celebrated by priests, bishops and even cardinals. During the procession of the Blessed Sacrament, I knew that miracles had occurred in the past. Imagine the feeling- not knowing if your life would be changed in an instant. I wouldn't know what to do if suddenly I were able to walk, if the Osteogenisis Imperfecti, which had ravished by body for fifteen years, had suddenly vanished. I was more worried about not fracturing while in France- what if the opposite occurred, and I was actually cured?

There was a common link there, I thought, looking over rows and rows of sick, handicapped, and dying people, of all ages. Some may have been more ill then others, some may have had more faith. Different cultures, different languages, different stories, different needs, and different expectations. All had sacrificed something to be together, at that moment in this holy place.

Perhaps there would be physical cures that afternoon, perhaps not. But all would leave with the message of Lourdes to share, especially for those not lucky enough to travel there. As Mrs. Feeley said "No one leaves Lourdes empty-handed".

In the evening there was a candlelight vigil. I vividly remember the singing of "Ave Maria" and the thousands of flickering flames sending millions of prayers to heaven. It was like being in another world.

"Go drink at the spring and bathe in its water", Our Lady of Lourdes had said. I would never forget the extraordinary opportunity I had to bathe in the miraculous waters of Lourdes.

After saying some prayers and kissing a statue of Our Lady, capable attendants into one of the stone reservoirs lowered me. Wearing nothing but underwear. Immersed in the ice-cold mountain water, I experienced a feeling never felt before or since. A surge went through my body like a wave of electricity, and a terrific pain knifed through my back. My fragile legs weren't completely submerged, and mom noticed this, and quickly splashed a handful of water over them almost immediately.

Afterwards I sat shivering outside the baths, in the summer sun, still in some pain and shock. But I dried amazingly fast, and remembered the encouraging words of Mrs. Feeley, that pain usually occurs before a cure.

Realistically, the pain I experienced was probably from the frigid water but until then I had always worn a corset for my back as a child, from the infamous vertebrae fracture some years earlier. But after bathing in the miraculous fountain at Lourdes, I threw away the corset. I never experienced back problems again.

We filled bottles and jugs to carry the precious Lourdes water home for family and friends. That afternoon we made The Way of the Cross, my parents pushing me up the rugged, steep hill near the Grotto. There was a smaller set of stations, especially for those who might have trouble navigating the high climb, but somehow we made it.

Another day we decided to cross the border and spend a day in Spain. After crossing the Pyrenees Mountains we became lost in a rainstorm, and somehow found our way back on the main road in the darkness and the rain. We felt strangely out of place after leaving Lourdes so we turned back and crossed into France again, so glad to see the towers of the basilicas in the distance. Like coming home.

Our last day in Lourdes was one of mixed emotions. We were homesick; I especially missed my Phillies, and got the scores each day from the French newspaper in town. Yet we were also sad to leave. This was a special trip, a special place, and we were so lucky to have come there. Who knew if we would ever return?

We were grateful for the chance to visit Lourdes, and I thanked my parents for bringing me there and especially for their sacrifice and love, which was just a continuation of their lifelong devotion.

We said our farewells to Mrs. Feeley and Brother Collins and the boys. We promised to write and most of all, to spread the message of Lourdes.

Then, for the last time, we kissed the smooth Rock of Massabielle, beneath the spot where the Blessed Virgin appeared, praying for a safe trip home, and that somehow, someday we would return.

Even on the return trip to America the power of Lourdes continued to shine. In customs at the airport, a tough-looking guard began inspecting or luggage. Tired after a grueling transatlantic journey, we didn't look forward to the anticipated wait.

Then the guard noticed our jug of Lourdes water. Would he take it away? Instead, he mentioned that even though he wasn't Catholic he had heard about Lourdes and asked about our trip. Good-hearted Mom, and also smart-thinking Mom, gave him a small bottle of water. He took it as if we had just given him gold. The burly guard was so overwhelmed in thanking us that he allowed us to pass through customs without delay.

In the ensuing years, much of the remaining precious water had served as a source of hope and healing, helping many that were sick and dying. Since our family and friends knew we had been to Lourdes many asked for a small sample of water when illness occurred. We were only too happy to share it.

Year later I met Pat Croce, former President of the Philadelphia 76'ers. I loved his positive outlook on life. I sent him a get-well card after his motorcycle accident several years ago. He replied with a thank you note, and asked to meet me at a future Sixers game.

Pat kept his promise and stopped by to say hello, even though he was so busy before the game. It just goes to show there are still nice people around.

In appreciation, I surprised him with a gift: a small bottle of Lourdes water, to help his recovery.

"You've been to Lourdes?" he asked with surprise. "Are you sure you want to give me this?"

It was as if I had just given him gold as well. He was so happy, writing me again later, thanking me for the precious holy water. Though I wasn't physically cured at Lourdes through my visit, I learned to accept my disability, not give up hope of ever walking, but acceptance. More importantly, remembering the words of Mrs. Feeley, I did not leave Lourdes empty-handed. Our Lady gave me a path to follow, a shining light whenever darkness surrounded me. Just as St. Bernadette devoted her life to caring for those in need, I, too, would find my vocation in life, helping others in need.

Now, some thirty years later, I look at the pictures of Lourdes, recalling the unforgettable memories. There is Dad, gone now, but a constant reminder of his love. There is Mom, still living and doing well, another memory of her lifelong love. And my brother Mark, now married with kids.

Someday I may return to Lourdes, with family or friends, or maybe alone. A voice inside keeps telling me to return, the same voice which has always guided me through life, telling me to never give up, to take my life one day at a time, and to make the best of what God gave me. It is the same voice, which compels me now to write my story. I am determined to listen to it, despite distance, disability or debt. It may be Our Lady of Lourdes, calling me home.

It was around this time in my life when we moved from my childhood home on Fourth Avenue to a small place on Hall Street, still in my beloved Phoenixville. Hall Street was where my Mom grew up. It was a smaller, cheaper house, but still three stories, so Dad would carry me up and down the stairs. I still wasn't very independent because my body was still fragile, but our house was also inaccessible. This move would be a major factor in my life later on.

I loved sitting outside in my wheelchair during the summer, playing Nerf ball with my brother and other neighborhood kids. And I had yet another crush, this time on a raven-haired beauty with sparkling lavender eyes named Sandy who lived a few doors away. She was a few years younger. She was cute, long hair, dimples. We would play cards together or I would help her with homework.

We were friends, but that old tingle ached my heart. I knew it could never be. Here I was, totally dependent in my care, not being able to drive (a big thing for teenagers); yet I wished to be like everyone else, especially during those low self-esteem years. I couldn't even get off the block to take her to the local movies if I wished.

It was tough, as Sandy grew older, and started becoming interested in guys. Less time spent with me. And I would sit outside on those warm summer nights and watch her get in a guy's car and drive away and I felt bad. Again I began to feel that life wasn't fair. I wanted to be a "normal" kid in a very not normal body and unusual lifestyle.

When we moved again, Sandy faded away, but she was already disappearing from my life, as so many would do. She married, had kids, and moved on with life, while it seemed my life was stuck in neutral- never changing, with any hopes to change.

My teenage years were also the surgical years. I was still fracturing, but I was alive, which amazed the doctors. So when I turned thirteen they decided to try surgery. I had five operations on my legs. Dr. Nicholson thought that inserting stainless steel pins and rods into the bones of my lower legs would not only strengthen the legs, but also hopefully allow me to stand and walk too, and keep the bones from bowing, which was beginning to happen.

But after each surgery, a few months later a scab would form on my leg. Soon, the shiny sharp point of the pin would be seen, protruding through the skin. My body rejected the pins and rods. Dr. Nicholson would then pull out the pins with a pair of pliers, and the process would start over again, with each surgery the pins were bigger, heavier, yet my body still wouldn't accept them.

It was frustrating for both Nicholson and me- going through all that work, pain, rehabilitation- to no avail.

Each time I had surgery, I dreaded to leave home. The day I left for the hospital was emotionally so painful, never knowing if I would see home again. Sure, the surgery wasn't life threatening, but to a kid, it was still scary. I spent most of my childhood at home, especially in my room, which was the center of my world. Leaving that warm environment for a cold, sterile hospital ward was traumatic in itself. The goal was always to go home. I could rehabilitate and get well again down the road, but the unfailing reward after each surgery was going home.

Very simple stuff, yet very powerful. I was never so happy as on the day I was discharged each time from the hospital. It wasn't that the care was bad. It was going home, to familiar food, familiar surroundings and most of all, familiar faces. I never appreciated home so much until I was away from it, even for a few days.

Two things occurred during this time: With each operation my legs grew smaller. They had to take bone out every time, so my legs became stunted. They were rounder, not as curved, at least until the pins rejected, but my legs looked like a dwarf, not in proportion to the rest of my growing body.

The first time they took off the cast after the initial operation, I was horrified. I never expected my legs to be so disfigured. They didn't look great before, with all the fractures, but now, I looked like a monster. I remember crying the first time I saw my legs after the surgery, and it was a terror I could never get away from.

It was during one of these rejection times that Nicholson and I had our first spat. Before, he would pull the pins out when they came through the skin far enough to grab. But the last time, the rods they used were huge. My legs felt weak, and I remembered the pain form past experiences. So when I got to the hospital I knew what to expect. And I totally lost it.

I wouldn't let Nicholson. -. Or anyone. -. touch me .I wondered why they could not numb my leg when they pulled out the rod. After all, one gets a shot of Novocain when one gets a tooth pulled, Here I was, having a steel dagger pulled out of the bone of my leg, and they didn't want to give me anything for the pain.

Dr. Nicholson's reasoning was, it would only take a second. Why go through the trouble of deadening the leg?

For the first time since I knew him and it had been close to ten years now, I felt he was out of touch with my feelings. I felt helpless on that cold table, begging them to help me. Please, don't make it hurt.

My parents couldn't do or say much. They tried to convince me to let Nicholson treat me, not to waste his time, and not to be such a baby and carry on. Be brave. I was made to feel guilty. I was trapped. I couldn't escape. I knew my fate, yet I didn't want to give in.

They finally had to hold me down as Nicholson grabbed the rod and gave it a yank. I screamed with pain. It felt worse then a fracture, which I was almost immune to by then.

I left the hospital in tears, my confidence shaken in my hero, Dr. Nicholson. I never wanted to see him again, and the thought of more surgery scared me more then ever.

When I stayed in the hospital during those surgical years, I still met many people- other sick kids, nurses, doctors. Often, interns or doctors from foreign countries would stop by my room to look at my legs. I didn't mind, although as I was growing older I was becoming more self-conscious about my appearance, as any teenager would. I wish I only had pimples to worry about.

At times I felt like an animal in a zoo, like an alien from another planet. But I had to remember I was a rare species, and anything to help others in my situation, to help the doctors understand O.I, the better.

One time they wheeled me into this big auditorium where I was greeted by a sea of white uniformed doctors and nurses. Nicholson was front and center, having various diagrams and x-rays tacked on the blackboard. He lectured for a while, showed the group my legs, and I was out the door again, much to my relief.

Even though the surgeries didn't help me to walk, as was the goal, the doctors were right about one thing- after age sixteen I stopped fracturing as frequently. That in itself was a miracle. Less pain, less trips to the hospital, fewer casts. I could live a semi-normal life. Plus it looked like I was going to live after all.

I was now officially wheelchair bound. I learned the fine art of doing wheelies and going everywhere at 100 MPH. I had an electric wheelchair at one time, but the doctors thought it was a good idea to stay with a manual, for the exercise. Plus the electric chair was cumbersome to put in the car. I got used to the chair, and would get a new one every few years, like trading in a used car (air conditioning was optional). To me, pushing my chair was like an able-bodied person walking, I didn't think about it, I just did it. Matter of fact, I guess that is how I approached most of my life, especially my upcoming college days. I didn't stop to think-I just did it. Maybe that was the best way, because if I stopped to think I may not have accomplished what I did.

With my legs now even more battered and scarred my low self-esteem continued to plummet. I became even more shy and withdrawn, Realistically, no matter the encouragement from family and friends; I knew I was different, at least on the outside. My legs were ugly. They always would be disfigured. It was a fact I had to accept and live with. It took a long time until I found peace in my heart and soul, as all I would have to do is look down at my legs and be constantly reminded of my past.

A few things helped to bring me out of my shell. One was C. B. Radio, which was the craze back then. I could be a normal kid, make friends and explore the world around me- without ever leaving home.

It was fun and I made a lot of nice pals. There was always someone to talk to, even in the middle of the night. I started going to radio-related parties and picnics. A whole new world was opening up for me.

A group of truck drivers found out about my situation, took up a collection, and bought my first radio. They hooked it up and installed the antenna on the roof. It was their way of spreading good cheer, plus helping me to reach out to others.

My first handle was "China Boy", because of my fragile bones. A lot of CB'ers would use a nickname or poke fun at themselves with their creative handles. My second handle was "Smitty", taken from my last name. Every male person in my family was called "Smitty'. When we all got together on a holiday, and someone shouted "Smitty!" numerous heads would turn. Plus the handle was a mini-tribute to my Dad, who was the one and only "Smitty".

My channel was channel 10. I hung out with people of all ages, but mostly kids my age, Catman, Wanderer, Skateman just to name a few. It was really the first time in my life I was part of a group of so-called "normal" people my age. On the radio, it didn't matter if one could not walk. Every one was the same. Race, creed, or in my case, disability did not matter.

We had occasional disagreements, especially with neighboring channels, and we broke a few FCC rules, like playing music on the air, or talking until the wee hours of the night without a break. But generally our group was fun, and I started to become popular on the air. I learned I had a sense of humor, and I could be myself.

I even had a few girls talk to me on a regular basis. There was Marnie, a cheerleader at a local high school: Irene, a tall, blonde Polish beauty with whom I developed yet another crush, and Kathy, a paramedic. She was special to me; her handle was "Micro-Medic" because she was tiny. We talked almost every night and became good friends. I guess I had a crush on her too, but knew she was dating a guy who was an intern at a local hospital.

We kept in touch, even after our radio days ended, and Kathy invited me to her wedding to the doctor, and now she has kids and leads a very happy life.

That is how it was on the radio- people came and went, fading away in time. On to other things. It felt like a club, but also like a family.

I also used the radio as a tool for doing some good. I soon got involved in Phoenixville's Town Watch program, and for a while every Saturday night I would spend a few hours as a base unit, keeping in touch with mobile units as they patrolled the streets, alerting police if they found anything suspicious. It made me feel like a part of the community, doing this volunteer work, and I was happy to be giving back something to people, a lesson not to be wasted later in my life.

It was always an interesting experience, meeting people from the radio. It was cool, putting a face to a voice. Some people were shocked when they met me, like "Wow, he really is in a chair!" Some of the girls were disappointed that smooth, cute voice attached to this small, brittle guy. But it also made me feel better, because people from the radio came in all shapes and sizes. I didn't feel so different.

I did miss a few things back then, like cruising. But the people on the radio more or less treated me like anyone else, including good-natured insults, which actually made me feel good, like I was part of the gang.

However, the radio was my first taste of discrimination as well. Soon, people found out about my disability, especially when my story made the newspapers about the truckers collecting for my radio. Most people on the radio didn't care about my disability. They looked into my heart and personality, as I wished everyone would. Some felt uncomfortable talking to me after that. That was OK-they weren't true friends anyway. But I learned later in life; most people are not cruel. They just may feel uneasy, afraid to hurt my feelings or say the wrong thing.

But there were people on the air who were just plain nasty and rude. They called me names like "crippled", especially in front of the girls, because I was taking attention away from some of these young punks. They threatened to find me, which wasn't hard to do, and dump me out of my chair, just for kicks.

There were two guys on the air who were especially cruel, Bob and Ray. Bob was a preppy dude near Valley Forge, a weirdo would who arrange meetings with people, then never show up, or scarier yet, would hang out unseen at the designated meeting place. Ray was a garbage man, and he often taunted me, one time parking at the end of my street and keying up his microphone every time I tried to talk, so I couldn't get through. That was his idea of fun.

Most of the time it was all trash talk and no action. But one just never knew if that person who is taunting you was a psycho or not. So I never picked a fight, and generally shied away from confrontation. That made the bullies seem even braver, until they met me in person. Then, I guess they felt kind of foolish, threatening a kid in a chair, and that just made them the target of embarrassment on the radio.

Luckily, I had enough good friends on the air to take care of me. But eventually I had to stick up for myself, but I was still pretty low in the self-esteem department. I would spend a few nights talking to my friends, and all it would take was one rude comment by a Bob or Ray, and I was back in my shell again.

I didn't know how to handle such ignorance. I took the comments to heart and cried a few nights to myself. I wouldn't sign on some nights, just to avoid the teasing. , despite the encouragement of my real friends, who threatened to find these jerks and kick their butts.

I wondered how people could be so heartless. If only they could feel as I did, to be in my position. Being disabled can happen to anyone at anytime. I felt trapped in my body at times, like here I was, a normal person inside, with this ugly body.

It took me a while to ignore those rude comments, just laugh it off, and try to find humor in such ignorance. But it still hurt. I didn't mind the names so much. The terms "crippled", "disabled" "handicapped". -. it didn't matter. The politically correct phrase soon became "physically challenged", but I was never one to make a big deal out of words. It hurt me more, to be treated differently and to feel like an outsider. Again, I was the alien.

In time I got used to stares in public. Kids would stare a lot, but actually I didn't mind because at least kids were honest. They would come up to me at the mall or elsewhere in public and sincerely ask, "What happened to your legs?"

I would briefly say something simple like, "Oh, I broke my leg," always with a smile. That satisfied their curiosity most of the time. I encouraged such questions in life because it let kids know I wasn't so different, and maybe they wouldn't be as afraid when they encountered the next disabled person. It made me deal with the stares and a smile often broke the ice.

Actually, adults were often worse then kids. They would stare too, but quickly look away, afraid to face the uncomfortable situation. Anything different was best ignored. Many times parents would drag their curious kids away and lecture in a whisper, "Shhh! Don't ask him things like that!"

I always felt that was the wrong approach. Just because adults had hang-ups about disabilities didn't mean that the next generation needed to feel that way.

Heck, even disabled people could be prejudiced too or stare at other people with differences. Just because I was disabled didn't mean I was a saint. I had feelings like anyone else, good or bad.

I'll never forget when I was in junior college and I talked to a professor about discrimination and prejudice. He was black, a friendly guy, intelligent. He became my friend and we would often chat after class.

One day he mentioned how I dealt with my disability, and he gave me some great advice, which I never forgot. He said that no matter how much he had achieved in life, all the honors and degrees he earned, the first thing people saw when he walked down the street was the color of his skin. Unfairly, often he was judged by his race alone. It was his cross in life, to have to prove himself to others, but this motivation just made him try harder to succeed in life.

He told me, I would need to do the same thing. No matter what I achieved, society would still judge me on my legs and wheelchair alone. That was the first impression people would have of me, and I had to learn to accept this fate and make the best of it.

The key was turning it into a positive, and allowing people to get to know the real me, my heart, my mind, my soul, the truly important parts of me. I wasn't really different after all. And he was right. Each time I encountered prejudice in my life, it only made me strive harder not to give up.

As other interests came into my life- school, girls, music, a job- I faded away from the radio as well. My "Leaning Tower of Pisa" antenna, famous for the way it leaned to one side, yet stayed on my roof for years, eventually came crashing down in our yard during a violent storm. That was the end of my radio days, but they were days I would never forget, important days that would help to mold me into the person I would become later in life.

3. PLEASE DON'T BE SCARED

Now that I graduated from high school, what next? I really didn't know what I wanted to do with my life. I did know that I just didn't want to sit around all day and waste away. Disability checks are great for those who need them, but I felt I had so much more to give, again my perception that I was more "normal" then what people gave me credit for. I didn't want to play into society's conception that a physically challenged person should stay at home and not work. Don't even think about having a girlfriend, or trying to lead a life similar to everyone else .You are different, and you need to stay away from everyone else. Just stay in your corner and don't bother anyone, don't make waves.

But that wasn't me. And I was never one to listen to society, anyway.

What was my calling in life? My passion? My destiny? I had no idea. I was always good at drawing and doodling from all the time I spent in bed, recuperating from fractures. I thought of becoming a commercial artist. I even applied for a "Draw Bambi" mail-order course. But soon I found the competition was tough in the art world, and unless one was truly talented, which I wasn't, I couldn't make a living at Art. Plus I didn't put my entire heart and soul into it. I don't know why. I still didn't have that burning desire.

Always having a love for sports. I thought about becoming a sportswriter. I contacted a local journalist to get his opinion. His reply was "Well, you really have to be able to get around." At least he was honest, and with enthusiasm, I probably could've pursued that field. But with discouragement from the onset, I became even more depressed.

It was just another trickle down factor of my O.I. The fact that I had a hard time choosing what I wanted to do in life. I almost had to let the profession choose me, to meet my abilities and yet consider whatever limitations I had. I mean, I was willing to try anything I really wanted to accomplish, but I also had to be realistic about what I could and could not do, plus deal with the pressures and barriers which society would put in my way.

Vocational Rehabilitation got involved with my case. They hooked me up with a special training program they were sponsoring with the University of Pennsylvania. The course was Computer Programming. It was funded by Vocational Rehab and the Wharton School, a really important business school. Not bad to have on my resume.

Back in the mid-70's computers weren't as abundant as they are today. It was a growing field and they promised a good-paying job at the end of the nine-month course.

I really didn't want to do it or wasn't interested. I knew I was more a people-person, never liked Math, and still didn't have that intensity. But what did I have to lose? I couldn't say no or else everyone would think I was a loser and really didn't want to work. I was stereotyped to be destined as "disabled" all my life. Despite my reluctance, I tried the course.

So each day Mom would drive me to a parking lot in nearby King of Prussia to meet a van with about ten other disabled people from around the area. It was like being in grade school again, but different. These students were all ages, not just in my age group. Some younger guys like me, a few older guys, maybe in their 30's or 40's. I imagine they were stuck in the rut of life, and this was their chance to break out, get a good job, make decent money, and most importantly, earn respect and independence.

I was still shy, and had a hard time making friends, even though again we were all in the same boat. They talked about what they would do after nine months, yearning for this chance to prove themselves. Me, I wasn't so sure. I was still pretty reluctant about the whole thing, and felt like an outcast, although later I realized that one can't sit back - if one wanted something bad enough- a job, friends, love- one had to reach out and grab it. I learned later in life; I had to be the outgoing one, the person who strikes up a conversation. I was still pretty isolated when it came to social skills, since I spent most of my youth at home or in hospitals. So even the basics, approaching someone for conversation, seeking friendship, was still hard for me to do.

I still wanted to make everyone proud. I hung in there for several months, but hated the course. Our professor was also disabled, a middle-aged guy named Alvin. He was brilliant, and despite the fact his body was racked with Cerebral Palsy. He sat in a wheelchair, wearing a suit and tie, and lectured. Every day, for eight hours. I hated the commute, picking up the van early in the morning, getting home late at night, studying in the evening, then having to do the same thing all over again the next day.

That was reality, that was life. Other people struggle the same way. For me, it was my first time in the real world. I had always been sheltered before, worrying more about my physical health than anything else. I wasn't supposed to even be alive, let alone worry about my future.

Math was still a problem. And the course was very dry. We didn't actually see or use a computer for weeks. I like my home computer now, ironically enough. I think if we learned on the computer it would have made more sense, instead of reading boring textbooks or listening to droning lectures. I needed something. or someone to spark a fire within my mind and soul. And it just wasn't happening.

After several weeks we took our first exam and I flunked it. I never failed a test before, and I was scared, no matter how hard I was studying and trying I just wasn't getting it. I hated the city, ate lunch alone, which was my fault, as my classmates would head outside, the younger guys talking about girls. That was still foreign to me, and it was funny because even though we all had some sort of disability, we were all different too.

I didn't want to be branded as a quitter, plus I didn't have another career to fall back on. I was depressed and couldn't see a way out. I continued to fail exams. My folks and family thought I was doing great, and happy that I was succeeding and would have a career after the course was over. Little did they know how I suffered. I was so afraid to tell anyone how I was truly doing. Again, I didn't want to be seen as a failure.

Even if I were lucky enough to slide through the course and land a job, would I really be happy?

I needed the Christmas holidays of 1976 to rest and get my thoughts together. I dreaded returning to school after the holidays. It was a terrible winter- bitterly cold, snowy, and the weather didn't make things any better, going to a place each day that I hated.

But just when I thought things couldn't get worse, they did, in a very unexpected way.

On New Year's Day of 1977 my Dad got very sick, complications from his lifelong battle with Diabetes. I remember how he stayed in bed that holiday, but since he wasn't getting any better the ambulance came and took him to the hospital. I remember watching in shock as they carried Dad down the stairs, as he had carried me every night, on a stretcher to the hospital. And it was the last time I would ever see Dad again.

Three weeks after he got so sick, he died in a Philadelphia hospital. It was always a bad sign when they had to transfer someone down the city. Sure, they had the best doctors there, but one knew it was pretty serious when the city was involved.

We got a call about 3:00 in the morning. We thought he was actually getting better, the infection in his foot healing. But it turned out that the infection had spread through out his body. His major organs were shutting down; Diabetes was finally winning after so long.

I heard the phone ring that night, awakening me. I heard my Mom downstairs saying, "He died?" I think she knew he had turned for the worse; She had just come form the hospital a few hours before and was planning on returning early the next morning. I heard her crying. Then a few moments later she looked in my room, saw I was awake, and said, "Daddy died".

Those words left me numb. I didn't think he was that sick. They never told me. I couldn't cry. I just lay awake the rest of the night. I thought of all the memories. How we went to ballgames together, to his Sunday night bowling matches. How he worked for all those years to provide for his family. What a great guy he is. Or was. And I wondered what would happen to me, to Mom, to our family. How would Mom be able to cope, not only with the loss of her husband, but now having to take care of me, and still raise the other kids who lived at home.

He was only fifty-five when he died.

I remember the day Dad was buried. It snowed at least a foot a few days earlier, a continuation of the terrible winter we were having. They had to struggle pushing my wheelchair threw the enormous drifts of snow at the cemetery just to reach the gravesite.

I still couldn't cry. People thought I was putting up a brave face, as condolences came. People stopped by the house. But in the end, late at night, we were alone. And reality set in, that Dad wasn't coming back. His favorite chair sat in the living room, untouched, just one reminder of him. But he was all around us. And late at night, alone in my bedroom I finally cried.

I would remember him in so many ways, every day of my life. But on special occasions he would be there. Like the day I did graduate from college. The day I got my first real job. And the day our Phillies finally won the World Series in 1980. Tears were in my eyes, not only from happiness but wishing Dad was there to enjoy the celebration.

Times like that, he was there.

I couldn't take it anymore. I decided to quit the course. I went down to Penn one day after the holiday break. I told them my Dad had died, and said I couldn't continue on. I received a good stern lecture from some lady at Penn. I didn't even know who she was, and didn't care. She was probably a bigwig at the school. She told me that I was throwing away a great opportunity, that I would never make anything of myself, that I was turning my back on everyone who tried to help me, including Vocational Rehab. After nine months, I would have a job, be making great money, and have independence in my life. Did I want to go back to being labeled as "disabled"? Back to a useless life of doing nothing? I was advised to think about it before finally decided to quit.

But in the end, I did what I thought was right at the time. I quit. Emotionally, I was close to a breakdown. I kept the door open that maybe some time down the road I would try again. Vocational Rehab was disgusted with me, but they kept my case open, reluctantly. They couldn't seem to understand what I was going through. The bottom line was, I was turning away form a career they had set-up for me, as they were paying all the expenses. If I wanted to sit home and rot, so be it. They tried, even if I gave up.

But in my heart, I didn't give up. I felt like a failure, a loser, and especially that I had let everyone down, including Dad, who always wanted me to be independent and had always believed in me. I hoped he would have understood my reasons and my feelings. I did try, hanging in there even after he died.

I just faced reality that I couldn't tackle this uphill battle any longer.

Somehow, that little voice inside reassured me that somehow, someway, everything would work out. I didn't believe that little voice, as I could see no way out of my box. People did care; they were trying to help me.

But it's funny how things work out. God and Dad had to be on my side. And even though my family, friends and Vocational Rehab were disappointed in me, Mom always remained loyal. Still, I was eased back into that old comfortable role of being disabled. "Don't worry, "she would reassure me. "You don't have to work. You will be alright."

She was right. Everything would turn out fine, in time. Those failures only served to make me stronger and more determined in life. And they didn't turn out to be failures after all, but triumphs. I couldn't see it then, but looking back on it, everything happened for a reason. Like pieces to a puzzle, everything fit. And as always, my hardships in life only served to make me a stronger person in time.

I had so many people who were very influential in my life- family, friends, even strangers- it would be nearly impossible to write about all of them. But one person who made a special impact on my life was my Uncle Henry.

After Dad died Uncle Henry became like my second father. He and my Aunt Sue lived in town. He was tall and thin, with glasses and a perpetual tan. He worked for many years at a local tire plant, as many of my family did- coal miners, factory workers. Immigrants from the old country who came to Pennsylvania, looking for work and freedom.

His passion was gambling, and he was happiest behind a card

table or at the racetrack. Henry and Sue argued often, over petty things, but that is how they lived- and loved- for over sixty years.

He would tell her to "Shut the hell up"- every other word out of his mouth was "Damn" or Hell"- which made Henry a salty character to be around- or he would half-jokingly threaten to "Throw her in the trunk" during one of our trips together. But overall he was a nice guy with a heart of gold, and they loved each other. As Sue said "He's like an antique- I can't get rid of him now."

Henry had an opinion about everything and wasn't afraid to express it, which was kind of refreshing. He didn't mince words, and although Sue was his leash, and advised him to "mind your own business", it didn't stop Henry from putting in his two cents.

Henry liked to play Blackjack in Atlantic City. He was good at the game, but better at Poker. But he held his own at the tables, told off the pit bosses, and led a fantasy Frank Sinatra type of life, his idol, dreaming of being a member of the "Rat Pack." He told stories in the car about Sinatra, along with his usual hunting and fishing yarns. I was a captive audience during our excursions to AC, but I found his stories interesting, like how he knew all the good fishing spots around Phoenixville, or how he once stayed in a tree for ten hours, waiting for a deer to pass by. His colorful language added to the interest and humor of his stories, and Mom and I laughed out loud many times during our trips with them.

Sometimes he told the same story twice and asked, "Did I ever tell you this one before?" Yes, but I didn't mind hearing it again, although Aunt Sue would groan in the back seat.

He literally had hundreds of stories to relate, and he liked me because I was a willing listener. At his older age, Henry was eager to share his tales and wisdom with anyone willing-or not so willing- to listen. It made his life complete, adding a sense of closure to his life, and made him feel that his life wasn't wasted, that he had lived a rich, full life. So, in that aspect, I think Henry enjoyed time with me almost as much as I looked forward to seeing him too.

He didn't dwell on my disability, but rather on my abilities, like playing Blackjack after age twenty-one, and that was refreshing to me. The only time he would mention my disability was in passing, and always commented to others "Hell of a shame, huh? He doesn't have any legs." (I did have legs, they were just short and stunted; Why Henry always thought I didn't have legs I never understood and never bothered to correct him).

The racetrack was also a favorite spot of ours. There was nothing like sitting outside, on a warm summer evening in Brandywine, Delaware, gazing at the programs, trying to pick a winner. Usually we didn't. But we tried. We followed a local driver (we liked to play the harness horses), named Wade, and when Henry saw that he was going to ride in the morning paper, he would call me up and ask if I wanted to go with him that night We both didn't have much money. Henry was only on his pension and social security, so we were $2 bettors, but we had fun. Henry hit it big once, hitting the Big E for over $2,000. But often we would be lamenting on the way home "We will get them next time."

We met baseball player Pete Rose at Brandywine once, and Henry wasn't afraid to go up to Pete when he spotted him in the clubhouse and ask him to say hi to me. So after the races were over, I waited near the doors as Pete rode down the escalator (with Henry behind him, beaming proudly with a wide smile). When he saw me in the chair, Pete stopped for a brief second, shook my hand, gave me his autographed photo and playfully rubbed my hair while asking "How ya doing, buddy?" before whisking out the door. And it was Henry that made it happen.

Henry was probably his best behind a Poker table He was a crafty one, a master bluffer, and played at all the local fire houses and church events. He could go hours without winning a hand, but at the end of the evening when the dust cleared Henry usually was a winner or at least broke even. He would lean next to me and whisper, after getting beat by a close hand "I'll nail him to the cross next time."

And most of the time he did.

Henry could be rude at times and forward and didn't care who was across the Poker table from him, even a priest, but he was admired and respected in town, especially by the older guys with whom he grew up.

After playing Poker for over sixty years, several times a week, Henry claimed to never have gotten a Royal Flush, the highest hand in Poker. The odds of getting a Royal Flush were high, but out of all the poker Henry played over the years, to not get even a single Royal Flush was unbelievable.

But he always chased that elusive Royal Flush- both on and off the card table. It kept him going in life.

I'll never forget the time Henry forgot Aunt Sue's lottery tickets. She played the same numbers each day. It was their 50th wedding anniversary, and she played 5017- 50 years and the date they were married, November 17th.

For some reason Henry forgot to get tickets that day and guess what? 5017 came up straight-$5,000 down the drain. It wasn't the end of the world, but pretty close to it.

Whenever they would argue from then on, Sue would make sure

she reminded Henry of the lottery incident, the final jab in the argument, a point that would haunt poor Henry for years.

Our fondest memories were coming home from AC and stopping at Pats' Steaks in South Philly for a tasty cheese steak at four in the morning. Henry was in his glory, chomping down a steak on the streets where "Rocky " was filmed. He grew up in the city, so he was familiar with this atmosphere and soaked it up.

We took many day trips together after Dad died, to New York, to visit relatives in New Jersey, or just an evening ride for ice cream. Each time I couldn't wait to spend time with Henry, because he was fun. You just never knew what he was going to say or do. He could be embarrassing at times with his language and bad manners, but most often he was a joy to be around, and Henry was the life of the party each time. A family event just wasn't the same without Uncle Henry.

Every family probably has an Uncle Henry. But I was sure no family had a guy quite like Henry in it.

Henry helped us out a great deal after Dad died. He was our handyman, and since he had a lot of time after he retired, when he wasn't fishing, he would stop by and fix a leaky faucet or whatever needed to be done. He often dropped off a basket of corn on the cob on our front porch, asking nothing in return. He took me under his wing, got me out, and wouldn't let me dwell on Dad or the hard times I may have been going through. He was fun, and he made me laugh. Henry, in his own clever way, knew what he was doing. Maybe he only went to sixth grade, but he had common sense, something people often lacked.

He liked a good football and baseball game, but he was happiest behind a card table, smoking one of his trademark cigars, which Sue couldn't stand, and the aroma lingered on his clothing. He ate bacon and eggs each morning, didn't care about his cholesterol, and drank beer in moderation.

Henry and Sue had one son, Eddie, a drifter who rarely held down a job and often was on the road or traveling between Las Vegas and home. He was leading the lifestyle Henry probably would've loved to lead, if he wasn't expected to be the breadwinner and family provider.

Edie wasn't home often; in fact, there were spans of years when Henry and Sue wouldn't hear from him. But he was still their son. And no matter what trouble he got into, or whatever failed endeavors or businesses he attempted to start during the years, they never let him down.

When Eddie got sick from stomach cancer and died, in his mid-50's it took the heart and soul out of poor Henry and Sue. Imagine, losing your only child, dying before you do. Sue was always the emotional one, and cried often. She took care of Eddie at home until he died. Henry was the strong stoic one, never showing his emotions. But after Eddies' death, Henry was quieter, like a piece of his heart was taken away, Eddie being a clone of his Dad. Henry would be seen at the cemetery during the day, crying before his son's grave.

There was a lot of guilt and regret after Eddie's death, and this time I was the one who tried to console Henry and Sue, and urged Henry to continue his card games, his fishing, his diversions in life. But I knew he wasn't the same, and never would be again.

We started worrying about Henry when he parked his car downtown one day-then forgot where he parked it. Someone called the police, and they located the car and escorted Henry home. One time, instead of pulling into the driveway of local church grounds for a card game, he drove into a field instead. He had showed up that night in our driveway without his glasses. I asked him where they were and he thought he had them on.

Sue knew about these episodes of forgetfulness and he probably forgot more then what she let on at home. But when Henry started to wander, and wouldn't eat, he went to the doctor, something he hated to do, was admitted to the hospital, and eventually to a nursing home. Ironically, he was a resident at the same nursing home where I would eventually work as a social worker. That broke my heart, seeing Henry waste away from Dementia, remembering the good times we had together over the years, trying to tell myself, the forgetfulness, the confusion, the occasional combativeness with the staff, wasn't the Uncle Henry I knew and loved.

Sue lost hope too, seeing Henry fade away, first mentally, then physically. He fell and broke a hip, then developed Pneumonia and died. He would remember me at times when I stopped down to visit him during the day. He smiled with a twinkle in his eye when we talked about Poker or having a cheese steak at Pats. He remembered the good times, but couldn't tell me what he did only five minutes earlier. It was so sad.

When Henry died it was like losing my father all over again. Sue didn't last long after Henry. She missed his companionship, even the times they argued, and she eventually shared his fate, ending up in a nursing home and dying after a few years.

An entire family wiped out, all in a matter of years. All the years of working at the tire factory, the beautiful home on Starr Street, everything was gone but the memories.

As a final tribute, I bought a new deck of cards, and placed them in Henrys' coat pocket as he lay in state. I scribbled the inscription on the

41

cards: "To Uncle Henry- May you find the Royal Flush in Heaven that you never found on Earth".

After Henry was gone, life wasn't as much fun. I still miss him. But I will never forget him, and how he made my life a little more cheerful, and most of all, made me smile.

After Dad died, Mom couldn't handle my care needs, especially the stairs in our three-story house. So she did a very brave, bold and bright thing- she sold the house. We moved into a new rancher across town. She used the money we got when Dad took an early retirement prior to his death. It wasn't the full benefits he would have gotten, but half was better than nothing, and it was enough to allow us to buy the rancher. Most of my siblings were now on their own, and without having steps to contend with, life would be easier for both Mom and me.

Some people thought she was crazy, selling the house, using the money from Dads' company. But she knew what she was doing, and it was a move, which would forever change our lives.

Things always happen for a reason. And if Dad didn't die, we may have never moved. And if we didn't move the pieces of my life puzzle, which I am ready to relate, may have never happened. Dad was looking after me, and after the fiasco at Penn, I firmly believed that he was guiding me from then on.

Without steps to contend with I slowly started to assert some independence. I learned how to toilet myself- no more bedpans- shower myself, with the help of a shower spray and shower chair, and now had the freedom to push my wheelchair all around the house, even outside if I wanted. It may seem like a small thing, but when you are so limited for so long, it was like being released from prison. I was no longer fracturing, so I felt almost "normal"- a whole new world to me.

Never take for granted, the ability to walk, or in my case, to push my chair, whenever and wherever I wanted to go, from my bedroom to the kitchen, to sit on the front porch on a summer night, to wheel out to the mailbox to get the mail or newspaper. I began to feel so much better about myself, both physically and emotionally.

There was a nursing home just a block away from our new house. I noticed an article in the local paper looking for volunteers. I had never been in a nursing home before. I didn't know what to expect. But I applied. I wasn't doing anything else, and instead of sitting around all day and doing nothing, at least I would keep busy and maybe help someone else too. That "little voice" inside, which guided me many times over the years, told me to visit the nursing home. So I did.

I worked in the gift shop and volunteered for several years, hoping to find my calling in life in the meantime. The gift shop was a fun place to work because I got to meet many of the residents who drifted in during the day to browse or buy the small items, which were offered.

One couple that came in daily was Bill and Dolly. Both were always dressed to the gills, like an old couple on top of a wedding cake, Bill wearing a suit, tie and hat, Dolly wearing a dress, heels and necklace. They weren't going anywhere, just walking up and down the hall, but it really didn't matter.

Bill thought he had worked with me about fifty years earlier, and he would often sit on the sofa in the gift shop and just shoot the breeze about our days working for the Pennsylvania Railroad. Dolly would patiently wait for him to finish. After a visit they would walk down the hall together, Dolly occasionally whacking Bill over his head with her handbag for no apparent reason.

I had to laugh sometimes, but it was also sad, to see the effects of age and Alzheimers. I learned that I could easily talk to older people, and enjoyed it, and they seemed to like me too. Maybe they trusted me because I listened, something few people did, and maybe because I was in a wheelchair, so they kind of knew I understood what it was like to need help and be somewhat confined.

The gift shop allowed me to meet a lot of the residents, and I became a fixture at the Manor, not only volunteering, but starting to work part-time doing odd jobs, like making posters for the Activities department, putting my art skills to good use. I must have made thousands of posters and signs over the years.

It gave me something to do, but more importantly, a purpose in life. I couldn't wait to get to the nursing home each day. When the weather wouldn't cooperate to allow me to push my chair the block from home to work, I was bummed.

One summer I was assigned to spend time with John. He was one of the residents, a friendly elderly gentleman who always dressed in western garb, a string tie and vest, always wearing brown, even though he grew up in Philadelphia. For some reason he often "neighed" like a horse. Out of pain or habit or both.

The current social worker and Activities Director thought it would be a good idea for me to visit John for an hour after I closed the gift shop at 3:00. They wanted me to try and strike up a friendship with John, who had a family, but they never came to see him. That was sad, even sadder then residents who had no family at all. I could only imagine the loneliness, the feeling of being forgotten, and the grief. The staff became surrogate families for those residents who didn't get any visitors, or maybe just saw familiar faces on holidays.

John and I became quick pals. I encountered him for the first time sitting in his wheelchair at the second floor nurses' station, head in hands, which was a familiar pose, dozing off as he waited for a cigar. When I introduced myself and shook his hand, he eyed me suspiciously with his sharp blue eyes, wondering what a "young fella" like me wanted with a forgotten old guy like him. Everyone else forgot him, so what did I want?

We started talking about anything- the weather, sports- anything to break the ice and find common ground. One thing John really enjoyed was reminiscing, so I allowed him to do most of the talking. I listened, which I found to be a very valuable tool in the future, and which most residents wanted-someone to listen to them.

John was proud to show me his grainy, yellow photos he kept in his pocket and under his leg, pictures of himself as a young man, his wife, his children, old cars, old clothes. He laughed at himself, musing "Didn't I look good back then?"

"I grew up in Philadelphia when Broad Street was a prairie" he laughed, in the nanny goat way of his. He stared at those memories for minutes at a time, wishing he could transport his aging, fragile body through the photos and back to his youth. Who knows what was going though his mind as he gazed at those pictures?

For me, it was fascinating, learning about the old styles of clothing, the different models of automobiles and houses. John's knowledge and stories were enjoyable, even though he tended to repeat himself often, and insisted on looking at the same pictures each time we met. To John it was closure, a way of validating his life, a chance to prove to himself that his life was indeed worthwhile. He was happy to finally have a listener-a captive one at that- and he reminded me of my times with my Uncle Henry. Who knew that those times listening to Henry's stories would prepare me for what was to come with my residents?

"My daughter!" he would simply exclaim. "What a great girl," he sighed, the words fading away like the faded photos. I knew it had to hurt him so much that his little girl now no longer cared.

Cards and cigars. John loved both. So everyday when I visited after closing the gift shop I would meet him at the nurse's station. He would have a smoke, almost crying like a baby when the nurse was late with his match. We would then head for the dayroom for some cards, John ordering some of the other residents who were either in his way or laying their heads on the round tables to "Beat it".

"Want to turn over a few?" he always asked when I arrived, bushy white eyebrows raised as he held up a pack of cards. It kept Johns' mind off other things and it was fun, the lone bright spot in his usual routine day. Our games made John happy, and I imagined happiness was at a premium for John. So I was only too happy to play along.

He taught me how to play Pinochle, or at least I thought it was Pinochle. One afternoon a nurse was watching our game and asked what we were playing. "Pinochle" I replied. "Why?" And she laughed.

"That's not Pinochle," she giggled. "I have no clue what you're playing."

As it turned out, neither did we.

Seems as though John got confused and had actually taught me versions of Pinochle, Rummy and Whist, all rolled into one. The blind leading the blind. Ah, no matter. We were having fun, which was the main objective.

When John caught pneumonia the following winter I visited him in the hospital. I brought him a box of his favorite cigars and a new brand new deck of cards.

"We will save these for when you get back," I encouraged.

"My buddy!" was all he said, looking at me with misty eyes, as he often did with his musty photos, with love. The nurses at the Manor informed me that on the days I couldn't make it over, John would lament about where I was and when was I coming to visit. He looked forward to our card games, talks and visits so much, more then I ever realized, and so did I.

John never made it back to the nursing home. He died that very night. Out of the hundreds of residents I would meet in the future I never forgot John. He was the first resident I met, the first I really made an impact with, and the first who changed my life as well. He gave me just as much as I gave him. He gave me a purpose to my life, back when my life was so confused and worthless. He allowed me to see that I could truly make a difference in someone's life, just by a simple hello, a kind word, or a few minutes to listen and care. That moment of happiness meant so much to someone so lonely.

He made me remember what it was like as a kid, lonely in hospitals, missing my own family, dependent on others. But most of all he showed me that, even though death hurt, it was a part of life, and that

45

the happy memories could never die.

He made me want to be a social worker. And when times got tough in school or work, I thought of John, and told myself not to give up.

Wheelchair Willie was one of my best friends from the CB radio. He was involved in a car accident several years earlier, which left him paralyzed from the waist down. He was a young, husky guy, cut down in his prime when he totaled his car on a rain-slicked highway. "Me and a tree had an argument", he joked. "The tree won."

He went through the usual stages of denial, anger, before finally accepting his situation. Once he did there was no stopping Willie. "Hell on wheels"- literally.

I always thought it would be tougher to suddenly adjust to a new disability. Sure, Willie had a taste of able-bodied life, which I never had, but I was used to my life, and didn't know any different.

I remember visiting a close friend back then. His name was Eddie. He was a lot like Willie- a real hell-raiser. Partying all the time, drinking. A big guy, good-looking, could have any girl he wanted. Lived life to it's fullest. Older then I was by about ten years. Our mothers were close friends.

Anyway Eddie dove off a diving board one summer at a public swimming pool. He noticed a little girl underneath him in the water. He twisted his body suddenly to avoid hitting her. Instead, he hit his head on the edge of the pool, breaking his neck. He was paralyzed from the neck down.

Despite the fact that I was in a chair all my life I couldn't imagine the tremendous grief and adjustment it had to be for Eddie. One moment a healthy, robust guy, the next a quadriplegic.

Now, everything had to be done for him. Feeding, bathing, toileting, dressing. His Mom took care of him. I used to visit him when I could, play cards, just talk with him, encourage and provide him with a source of understanding.

But no matter how hard I tried Ed was still depressed. He could never fully accept his fate, nor could he ever bring himself to be a fighter and want to get better, like Willie or actor Christopher Reeve. He just gave up.

And that's how it was. At age twenty-eight, Ed died. There were complications from his condition- bedsores, pneumonia. But basically he lost the will to live.

So I was lucky, in a way. I didn't give up. And I was doing the best I could with my life. I wasn't totally happy with my life, and knew God had other plans in store for me. I just didn't know what they were back then. But I never gave up .Yet I could see how easy it would have been to give up. I could even understand why people did lose faith.

Willie didn't pout or sulk with his new lifestyle. It was like a nightmare for a while, a dream he could never wake up from. But he couldn't suddenly make himself whole again, so he decided to do the best he could with what he had. In fact he was everything I wanted to be- a role model. He drove a specially equipped revved-up green van with a hydraulic lift and hand-controls With his other car, a beat-up Chevy, he just climbed into the driver's seat, throwing his wheel chair into the back seat, and took off.

He was going to college to become a social worker .He also had independence, another thing I hungered for. He wasn't above getting under his van to fix it or plopping out of his chair to the dirt to garden. He reminded me of everything I was missing in life- shooting pool, wheel chair basketball, picking up girls. He showed me that I was limiting myself by thinking I was really handicapped.

So, in many ways I wanted to be like Willie. In some ways I did not, like the time Willie strapped himself in his chair and used himself as a human sled down a snowy hill. What I admired most about Willie was his fierce determination and will to enjoy life. He came so close to death. It took the accident to make him live life to it's fullest.

He knew how much I loved working at the nursing home. He put the idea in my head that I could actually get paid doing what I loved to do.

I didn't know what social work was, or what a social worker did for a living. I remember doing some research about social work- the academic qualifications, the salary. I knew I needed to attend college for at least four years, earning my Bachelor's degree, in order to get a decent job in the field A Master's degree was preferable and would give me more options in the field, plus more money. But one step at a time, and a Bachelor's degree was the first hurdle- and that meant four years' of college ahead.

Did I really want to do it? The time, the expense, the dedication? I sought advice from the current social worker at the Manor. I'll never forget his answer.

"You'll never make a lot of money in social work, "he replied honestly, "but some things are just more important then money".

47

I did have the desire, the determination, especially after the University of Penn debacle. I wanted to prove to everyone, myself included, that I wasn't a failure, not a loser. That I didn't need to be on disability all my life. God gave me a reasonably good mind, why not use it? I knew I had so much more to give, then just sitting at home all day.

I was angry too, and determined to attack my studies with all I had. I wanted to prove a lot of people wrong, wanted to award people, like mom, who always had faith in me, that she wasn't wrong. I wanted to make dad proud.

I wanted to show Vocational Rehabilitation I could do it. When they heard of my dream, they were even a little leery. I threw away a potentially great career once, would I give up again?

I needed help, with grants and loans, I was only working part-time at the nursing home, because I didn't have any skills to hold down a full-time job. Plus while I was on disability benefits I couldn't make much money. So I needed help to buy textbooks, and money for gas to get back and forth to school.

So I took the first step to college. I applied for every grant and student loan I could find. A lot of red tape, a lot of time spent doing paperwork. But to me, it was worth it. The toughest step was just saying I wanted to try, after settling into a comfort zone of doing nothing with my life. When I brought up the idea of college, eyebrows were raised. College? No, not for Greg. He can't do it. He already showed that he can't do it .Let him try, but hardly anyone thought I would stick with it.

There was one main difference between college now, and my days at Penn. This time I wanted to go to school, I wanted to make something of my life, and I liked the idea of becoming a social worker, to help others in need. I already knew what a difference I could make in someone's life, as I had with John, and I craved for the opportunity to do more in the future .I yearned for the respect and dignity which a degree would give me. A degree would allow me to seek a good job, but equally as important, a degree would change my life and allow others' to look at me in a different light. It would also give me the self-confidence I needed to excel in life, in all aspects of my life.

So I decided to go for it.

The plan was to carpool with Willie, since his classes were similar to mine He was a semester ahead of me, but his time on campus was practically the same as mine, so it would work. I appreciated Willie for the fact that he cared. He had been there before, on both sides of the fence. Able-bodied and disabled. A client and now a caseworker. He understood my life as few people could.

Mom wasn't too thrilled with the fact I would be carpooling with Willie each day. He was reckless, swore often, and still drove too fast. But he was the fun, beer-guzzling, independent guy I needed in my life, to bring me out of my shell. It started with the CB radio, but now, Willie was physically encouraging me to get out in the world more.

Life was too short, as I knew so well. I had survived my childhood, when doctors didn't think I stood a chance. God gave me a second chance to live. Now it was up to me to take advantage of that chance.

My first day at the Montgomery County Community College in Blue Bell, PA was also my very first day in a "regular" school with able-bodied students. It was a big adjustment I had to get used to a desk, lockers, traveling, a blackboard, and a teacher in front of me, changing classes on the fly. It was tough enough adjusting to college life, plus I had all of this other stuff that people usually take for granted to get used to.

We went to a community college because as Willie explained, it would be a good start, to see if I really wanted to pursue my goal of being a social worker. Plus, it wasn't as expensive as a big university. I had to get back into the routine of studying again, taking exams, and college life. I still worked part-time at the nursing home, trying to supplement my disability checks with as little money as I could squeeze out, most of it going back to college expenses. Mom didn't have the money to help me much, and Vocational Rehabilitation helped me, to a point. They wanted to see how I would do during my first semester, and before investing in me again, wanted to make sure I wasn't fooling around anymore.

So I did it the hard way. But that's what makes the ultimate goal that much sweeter to achieve.

I took six classes that first semester in the fall of 1984. Eighteen credits. Was I nuts? I loved my courses, especially my social work and psychology courses, but all I did was study, and attend classes. A typical day was classes starting at 8:00am and not ending until 10:00 at night. I would come home, study, catch a few hours of sleep, go to work the next day, study some more, then prepare for the classes the next day. That was my life, and I poured my heart and soul into it.

I took time to have fun too. Sports, music and friends were in my life. But this was my shot, maybe a once in a lifetime chance and I wasn't going to blow it again.

Making friends was an adjustment as well. Especially able-bodied friends. Often I ate lunch alone, too shy to approach others. I had to quickly learn that as a disabled person, someone seen as "different" I was the one who needed to introduce myself, proving to others that I wasn't so different after all.

Later in life, even at work, when no one would sit with me in the lunchroom, or sit beside me in a seminar, I had to force myself to take the first step. That usually broke the ice. But it was hard; being shy, to make that first step, which is always the hardest.

Unlike my days at Penn, I learned to make friends and tried to be more out-going. I noticed the more forward and sociable I became, the easier it was to make friends. Unless someone was really special, few would ever come up to me and offer to have lunch or study together. I had to make the initial move, and I learned this would be true through out my life.

Pretty soon, even my friends admitted that my chair was almost "invisible". I was seen for the person I was- for my mind and heart, rather then just my legs alone.

To my surprise I aced all of my classes that first semester. I was as surprised as anyone was. I didn't think I was stupid, but then again, I was no rocket scientist either. So I was trying hard and achieving, through hard work and determination, or college wasn't as hard as I thought it would be.

After that first semester eyes opened. Was it a fluke? Vocational Rehabilitation was now willing to help me more financially, which I was more then grateful to accept. It's one thing trying to help yourself and doing it the hard way, but it's another thing to accept help when it's offered, and be smart enough and humble enough to accept it. People had helped me all my life, for which I appreciated their kindness, why should I suddenly have an ego or attitude and say no? I needed help, so I wasn't bashful when someone offered to make my life a little easier.

Most of all, the great first semester made me believe in myself. My confidence soared. I wanted more. I couldn't wait for the second semester, to learn more. I wanted to feed off the success I was achieving. I actually started to believe that someday, maybe, I would graduate and earn my degree. But realistically that was a long way off, with many more mountains to climb. So I didn't want to get too full of myself just yet. I needed to stay hungry and determined. What worked the first semester should work during the second.

I tried not to stop and think too much. If I actually thought about what I was doing maybe I wouldn't have continued. Maybe I would've caved in to the doubters.

So I just did it. From class to class, test to test, term paper to term paper. I didn't slow down, even during holiday break and summers. I just kept pushing ahead, like I was pushing my chair through the snow, Full stream ahead.

I survived through bad weather, snowstorms, pushing my way across campus, having my history book stolen, and the embarrassment of once dropping everything. -. Papers, textbooks, personal items, right in the middle of campus as I was rushing to a class.

But I always found there were people willing to help. My view of society changed. People still cared. They may have still looked at me differently as a physical person, but I still encountered kind hearts along the way. I didn't refuse, when someone offered a push, or to carry my books. I learned to graciously accept assistance. I didn't take it personally. Just like it really didn't matter if someone put a label of "crippled" or "handicapped" on me. As I was getting out in the world I would encounter prejudice but I would also find humility and genuinely good people.

I made new friends, joined a few clubs on campus, although I didn't have much time between my studies, and really enjoyed school. I think it was an advantage to be an older, returning student. I was twenty-eight when I started college. I was there for a purpose, and although I was never one to pass up on some fun, I always kept my ultimate goal in mind. Making new friends was gravy, and important, especially since I was always socially isolated in my past. But the prize was graduating.

Then another twist occurred, one I never expected- Willie quit school. He was having more physical problems. But instead of taking a semester off, he dropped out completely.

How ironic! He was the one who encouraged me to go for my degree. He was my role model, the guy I aspired to be someday. But he was the one who quit, while I hung in there. I don't know why I stayed, but I did.

Later, in years to come, I learned that Willie resorted back to his old ways, drinking, doing drugs, no job, getting in trouble with the law, even spending time in jail. A guy in a wheelchair behind bars? It only proved that we are only human.

I felt like I had lost a friend- but reality said I also lost my ride, my transportation to school. Forget the inspiration, the encouragement-how was I going to get to school now?

I put an ad on a bulletin board at school, hoping for a miracle. Good-hearted Mom took me back and forth for a while, a distance of about 30 miles each way. She sacrificed as much as I did, getting up early, driving through bad weather, and picking me up late at night. I felt bad for her, and was tempted to quit, just to save her from this hardship.

But she always encouraged me to keep going, to never stop, that everything would work out in the end.

Luckily my prayers were answered and I met an angel named Laurie. She was also majoring in Social Work. She was a single mother of two kids, and had her own unique story. She was divorced, on welfare once, got herself together and decided to get her degree as well, to make life better for herself and for her kids.

She was independent, a free spirit who grew up in California during the late sixties, a flower child. She made me laugh, and we became good friends. There was never any romance involved, no crushes this time. That was OK with me, as I looked at Laurie as an older sister, again someone I admired a great deal for her guts.

Since she was taking almost the same classes as I was, she saw my ad seeking a ride and asked if I wanted to carpool with her. She went out of her way a few miles to pick me up, but she didn't mind. That was Laurie.

My Mom trusted her, as she had a good sense of humor, laughed easily, plus was older, maybe in her 40's, so she knew what she wanted in life. She smoked, and we laughed a lot, and we would quiz each other in the car on the way to school before a big test. We both motivated each other, and I think I helped her to hang in there too, as I know she admired my strength as well.

We would carpool together for the next four years, always friends, best buddies, even after we parted ways after graduation. If there was ever a scenario for true friends, it was Laurie and I. We were meant to meet, and it felt like destiny, like a missing piece of the puzzle, someone to always remember.

So I was starting to come out of my shell in the 80s'- in more ways then one.

4. SWEET HEAVEN (I'M IN LOVE AGAIN)

Singer/Songwriter and superstar Barry Manilow would play a big part in my life in the years to come. I had always liked his music. Bobby Rydell would always be special to me, getting me through many dark times as a kid. But then Barry came along in the seventies. Again I was going through some tough times, With my Dad dying, my continuing fight with brittle bones, and my failure in school. I needed some cheering up, and Barry's music was always there for me.

His music encouraged me never to give up. Being the hopeful romantic I am, I especially loved the soft ballads (the ones the critics hated), songs like "Could It Be Magic" and "Tryin' To Get The Feeling". His music was like a friend, always there when I needed a lift. It was music to listen to late at night, music to cry to, to smile with. Barry was writing and singing about emotions, which I could relate to, experiences happening in my life. Inspirational songs such as "All The Time" and "I Made It Through The Rain", with lyrics about not giving up hope, kept me hanging in there.

I saw Barry for the first time in concert at Resorts in Atlantic City, a familiar site, with my brother Pat and his soon-to-be wife, Linda, who was also a fan. We were in the back row, Row Z, as far back as we could be, but I was just happy to be there.

For a guy, it may have been not so cool to like Barry Manilow's music back then, but I didn't care. I appreciated his music, and like always, didn't really care what other people thought.

I wrote for a pen pal during the summer of 1984, writing to the Barry Manilow International Fan Club (the BMIFC for short). The club had just started a new program matching Manilow fans from all over the world. The goal was to make new friends and share in the music, something even strangers from different lands had in common.

When I read about the program in the summer newsletter I decided to join. I didn't know what to expect, and never had a pen pal before, but said "Why not?"

I had originally joined the fan club in 1983. I met many great friends through the club over the years, some local and some far away. Now I was hoping to find another friend in my pen pal, someone that loved Barry's music, someone to share stories and memories with.

When I wrote to express my interest in a pen pal, the BMIFC

wanted to know a few things in return. What were my interests and hobbies? Was I looking for anything special in a pen pal? No, but I was hoping for someone outside of America, looking to broaden my horizons a bit. Other then the pen pal being able to correspond in English, I asked for nothing more.

I listed my age and a little biographical information. Chances were pretty good that my pen pal would be female, since the majority of Manilow fans were female. But romance was not my intention. I was seeking friendship to help ease the lonely hours, never dreaming how things would eventually turn out.

Even before I received my first letter I had a decent idea of what my mysterious Manilow pen pal would be like. I'm not one for stereotypes, but generally, Manilow fans tended to be friendly, sensitive people, taking after the music they love.

Little did I know but at the same time a young woman named Liv-Karin was also writing for a pen pal through the club. She was twenty-five, from a small town in Norway called Larvik. She was single and attractive, a second year law student at the University of Oslo. She had been a devout Manilow fan since the early 80's especially after she saw Barry in concert the one and only time he played in Oslo. Liv had middle row seats, since she was the first person in line for tickets. Of course, there were only two other people in line, and they were both Americans.

Barry was not well known in Norway back then. Liv heard of his early hits, like "Mandy", over Armed Forces radio, which broadcast a weekly Top 40 show to Oslo. She fell in love with his music and soon she was scouring music stores in Oslo for any Manilow albums she could find. Albums were not imported easily, so there wasn't much of a selection.

After Barry's successful 1983 concert in Oslo the records became a bit easier to find. Liv joined the fan club and the rest was history.

She wrote for a pen pal on a whim. She already had a pen pal in Sweden, nothing to do with Manilow, just the writing kind. But as it turned out we had more in common then we could imagine. Both around the same age, both struggling students, both from small towns. Larvik was similar to Phoenixville, quiet, tree-lined; with friendly people and basic small town traditions- only Larvik had an ocean.

Our interests and personalities were even similar: sensitive, caring, and romantic, easy-going, fun. The fan club did an uncanny job of matching up two people from opposite ends of the world.

Best of all, we were Manilow fans. Not fanatical, obsessed with Barry every waking moment, just loyal, die-hard fans. We were the fans who waited in line for tickets for hours: who bought all the albums and tapes; who clipped out newspaper articles and taped television performances religiously; who especially loved the "little" songs tucked away on each album, songs which never made it to radio.

We were the fans who appreciated each lyric, who were the first to buy a new record (even before they were taken out of the box), who just loved Manilow music more then anything.

When I wrote for that pen pal during the summer it took a while for an answer. With college beginning soon I forgot about the pen pal application, which was winging its way to the fan club headquarters in Los Angeles.

Maybe my letter was lost? Or maybe the fan club decided to abandon the whole thing? Whatever the reason, I never gave it a second thought until one early day in November.

The letter from the fan club read,

Dear Greg,

Thank you for your letter. We've received quite a few letters from members wanting pen pals; we're glad you'd like to have one.

Now, as we mentioned in the last newsletter, this isn't the dating game. We've tried to match everyone up who wrote in to the best of our abilities, but it isn't always possible to find the pen pal of your dreams. We hope we've come close, but in case we haven't, give it a try anyway. You never know...you may find someone who turns out to be a lifelong friend!

Good luck and have fun...

I had Liv's name and address. The rest was up to me. I knew little about Norway; the typical American who thinks Norway is the capital of Sweden. I had so much to learn.

I almost didn't write that first letter, even after receiving the address. First letters are so hard to write. Still, I sat down one evening and tried to introduce myself the best I could. It was difficult writing to a complete stranger, to someone in a foreign country.

I described what I looked like- short, dark hair, bluish-green eyes, and the infamous dimples- up to a point. I left out the fact that I was disabled.

I was still too insecure to admit my handicap, which made it even more of a handicap, believing that if Liv knew I was disabled she may not write back, as if being disabled was against some international pen pal law. After being hurt in the past I didn't have the courage to be truthful. Too many times I had made 'friends" who had ended up judging me solely by my twisted legs instead of my heart.

I wasn't being fair to Liv or to myself. Why should my disability matter, especially to someone I may never meet anyway?

It didn't matter but I didn't know that then. For now I kept my disability a secret.

I wrote about Manilow music and how I joined the fan club, listing my favorite songs and albums, sharing my feelings of why I liked each song and what made each album so special.

I tried to keep that first letter short and sweet, yet somehow it ran nearly ten pages in length. I had so much to tell her, and after the boring introductions, the letter turned out to be fun to write. I signed the letter, "Your Pen pal, Greg," stuffed it in an envelope and dropped it in the mail.

Waiting is always the hardest part. Would I get an answer? Calm down, Greg. It's only a letter and she is only a pen pal.

It was two weeks later when I received a reply. She was funny, warm and friendly, like I had known Liv forever. Her letter was fantastic, better then I could imagine. I wasn't used to being treated so well, and I loved how her personality shone through those initial pages.

She wrote of her hometown, her life, and her dreams. She was 5'3 (whatever that is in the metric system), slim, with shoulder-length blonde hair and blue eyes (what else from a Scandinavian?).

She was a law student, struggling in her tuition, but not in her studies. Her financial situation sounded very familiar.

As I learned more about Norwegian culture I would admire Liv even more. Women in Norway are usually advised to be nurses, secretaries or housewives. Very stereotypical views. Not Liv. She had the courage and determination to break the mold, and I could relate to her rebellious nature against society.

For now, just paying the rent on her apartment at school was the most important concern to Liv. That, as well as passing the rigorous exams at the university. Two more years until she earned her law degree.

Liv's father had also died when she was a child. On weekends and holidays she would take the train home. She lived there with her mother, who worked as a gardener. Soon I grew familiar with Liv's family- an assortment of uncles, aunts, nephews and nieces, plus a fourteen-year-old canary named Rudi. They became very real to me, as my family did to her.

We learned that we each loved old black and white movies, parks in springtime, trivia games, quiet evenings at home, and Italian food. Most of the letters were about Manilow, as when Liv told me about the Oslo concert. She was in the front row, so close to Barry that she could almost touch him. In fact, during his "Can't Smile Without You" segment of the show, when he picks a member of the audience to sing with him on stage, he looked right at Liv and asked, "Do you want to come up here?"

While Liv stammered in disbelief Barry picked someone else. A chance at stardom down the drain.

Those first few letters were so fresh and new. They made us feel like somebody out there understood and cared. We reached out for a friend and found one. We were both dreamers, wishing on a star, knowing that somewhere out there, someone was wishing the same wish. Just didn't know that special person would be an ocean away. Out of all the people in the world, what were the odds that two people from so far away, from different cultures and background, would find each other?

It was all pretty amazing to me. I loved it, and since I never had many friends growing up, I loved this new experience.

As the months and pages went by we became even closer. I couldn't wait for two weeks to pass until I received another letter from Liv. I spent long evenings writing back to her, some nights past midnight, in between my studies. I would read her letters over and over until a fresh one arrived.

It was a surprise that Liv was feeling the same way. She couldn't wait for my letters either. We joked that it was a shame that we were so far apart; we could talk for hours if we had the chance. We shared secrets and dreams, slowly becoming best friends as well as pen pals.

How could we grow so close with pen and paper alone? Maybe we were just meant to find each other, despite the vast distance between us. There was a bond growing with each page. It felt wonderful to care about someone, and finally, to be cared about.

Another crush? Maybe. But it felt so much different then the past. How strange, since I never met Liv, yet I felt closer to her then anyone in my past.

In December Liv sent a Christmas card, the first of many to come in the years a head. It read: Greetings from your pen pal!" But the cards didn't stop there. We sent greeting cards and post cards between our regular letters, with wishes like "Thinking of you" and "Wish you were here." One I will always remember had a glowing, romantic full moon hovering over a dark ocean, with the simple words "Miss you" on the front.

Writing to Liv now became such a big part of my life. She became a big part of my world. I couldn't imagine life without her. Life would be so empty and meaningless.

I listened to songs like "All The Time", of finding someone after so long, and felt what a shame we were so far apart. We discovered each other's heart first, which was a novel way of getting to know each other, the most important place to start any relationship.

The word "relationship" was out of the question. We were strictly pen pals, and the crazy thought that we could ever be more was so unrealistic that any such ideas were quickly dismissed. I couldn't let my dreams run away with my head. It could never be.

We started adding little surprises to our letters- Manilow posters, articles and tapes. Everything we discovered concerning Manilow had each other in mind.

I began searching for books on Norway, reading all I could about Norwegian culture. Towns such as Oslo and Trondheim became familiar places, foreign no longer.

Overseas, Liv was taking an equal interest in America. She didn't need as drastic a crash course in lifestyles as I did. America had always been special to Liv. It was her dream to visit the States someday, especially New York City. She was well aware of the crime and grime, the traffic and crowds, the muggers and homeless. But she viewed New York and all of America as an outsider would, as maybe we all should, as an exciting, romantic hopeful, wonderful place to be.

During this time Barry released his jazzy: 2:00 AM Paradise Café" album. There was a smoky atmosphere to that record, a feeling as though one is sitting in a lonely café late at night, listening to beautiful, bluesy ballads, while the autumn rain falls softly outside. It was an album for lovers, an album to share with someone special. We rushed out and bought it that chilly winter, the warm music melting those long, cold evenings alone. Although we compared favorite songs, there was an aching feeling inside our hearts that there could be so much more, if only...

As the New Year drifted by I picked up a few hints of Liv's caring. I recalled her description of what it was like when she received one of my letters.

"I don't even wait for the lift (elevator). I run up the stairs, my heart pounding, sit down on the edge of my bed, tear open the envelope, and read your letter over and over again..."

Wow!

The letters made us laugh, cry and dream. They also made us realize there was a pretty unique person across the Atlantic, like no one else in the world.

It was so frustrating. Here was someone I had been waiting for all my life, yet I couldn't be with her. It didn't seem fair. We were closer then couples who were together all the time, yet we were still so far apart. But I counted my blessings that I had found Liv. If it was meant to be only friendship, then so be it.

As the months breezed by I knew it was time to explain about my disability. It hurt when Liv mentioned that one of her favorite things to do in the summer was to climb the hills overlooking Oslo and the sea. She invited me to join her someday to share the view. How I wished I could.

Then I got Liv's picture. She was pretty, petite and tanned, with glistening golden hair, sparkling sapphire eyes and a sunny smile. It was more then just a crush-I was in love.

I never experienced that special feeling before. . I just knew it was different. I was already in love with Liv even before I saw her photo. It made the heartache even worse. Every time I looked at her it was a dream of what could never be.

She lived too far away. It would never work. Why ruin a good friendship? After all, she still didn't know my secret.

We were just two ships that passed in the night every two weeks or so, doomed to go on living in different continents. We would find someone else someday, settle down, get married, have kids and grow old-apart. At least I was sure Liv would realize those dreams. In my situation, I wasn't so sure.

I knew I was in trouble when I couldn't get her out of my mind. Did Liv have a boyfriend? Liv was engaged once to her childhood sweetheart. Things didn't work out, as they became "too good of friends". He eventually married, while Liv concentrated on her studies. She dated now and then, but there was no one special in her life.

"So you see," she wrote, "there will be no jealous boyfriend when we go on our tour of New York together."

Tour of New York? Oops. . I forgot to mention New York. Since New York City was Liv's city of her dreams, I conveniently suggested that if she ever came to the States I was just the guy to show her around the Big Apple.

Wrong! I had trouble getting off the street corner in my wheelchair let alone New York.

My heart ran wild, especially after Liv described her "dream date": a walk through Central Park, a tour of Manhattan. A Manilow concert, then a quiet, candlelight dinner for two in a cozy Italian restaurant, with good food, a glass of wine and then…dessert.

"Wanna join me?" she asked.

No wonder I had lost all common sense. That old friend of mine, the romantic fool, took control again. How could I say no? I was too far-gone to turn back. I didn't mean to lie, to lead her on. I was confused and didn't know how to get out of it, even if I wanted to.

It was agony, wanting to meet her so much, yet by doing so, having to face the truth about my disability. Yet it was ecstasy too, having Liv in my life.

Music, friendship and love melted the many miles between us. There was so much to love about Liv. She was an old-fashioned girl; stubborn at times but loyal. There was no one like her-literally- in the entire world, and as the cards and letters continued, I began to realize just how special she truly was. Soon distance and disability didn't matter. I had to meet her.

I heard of other pen pals meeting, some even marrying, and my hopes soared. Despite the many obstacles in our way could we have a relationship? Should I risk being hurt- or being happy?

We exchanged gifts that Valentine's Day. Liv sent me flowers while I sent her a "Teddy Barry" Suddenly we weren't just kidding anymore about meeting someday. Liv said that with hard work over the next year she might be able to save enough money for a vacation in the summer of 1986.

It was a long shot plan, something to look forward to. Liv continued to invite me to Norway to share the upcoming summer. There was so much she wanted to show me: the famous Sculpture park, the Viking Museum, the many quaint sidewalk cafes and shops dotting Oslo. The mountains and fjords- and those hills overlooking the sea.

I wanted to say "yes" and go. I wanted to meet Liv so much. Then something unexpected happened.

There was a postal strike which cut-off all international mail. Was Liv all right? What if I never heard from her again? I was so used to her wonderful letters, then to suddenly lose her.

I was miserable for a month, checking the mailbox, only to find it as empty as my heart.

Finally our letters came through and it was the first time we wrote, "I love you". Those lonely weeks out of touch gave us a taste of life alone again. We were determined never to let go.

Before any plans for a summer together were finalized I had to tell Liv the truth about my physical limitations. I wanted the message to be personal, so I sent Liv a tape, recorded on a late spring evening. I explained everything, about the fractures and hospital stays, the surgeries and long days of rehabilitation. I told her about the loneliness, the prejudice, the pain, and the happy times too.

I told her that I was better, not fracturing as often. I told her about the wheel chair, and the fact that I was now trying to lead a normal life, going back to school. I had not achieved total independence yet, but I was trying.

If Liv changed her mind about our relationship I would understand. Our relationship was a bit unusual. But there was also so much to build on. And I didn't want to lose her.

Liv could find another "special someone". The sensible thing for her to say would be "Let's go back to writing letters- nothing more, as we started". Why would she want to get involved with a guy like me?

I braced myself for her next letter. I got another postcard from Liv first, saying that she loved and missed me, and a letter would follow. Did she send the card before or after she learned the truth?

I hesitated before opening her letter this time. It turned out that Liv was surprised, of course, but her feelings didn't change. In fact, they were stronger. She admired my courage for finally telling her. Sure, she had some normal questions: How did I get around? What, if any, special needs did I have? Was there a chance I could ever walk again?

Those questions were easier to answer now, and for the first time in my life I faced my disability without fear.

Liv had a surprise too. She had an eye problem as a kid. Luckily the problem was correctable. But she still remembered the long hours of therapy and the occasional teasing from other children. She could understand my feelings and anxiety.

She still loved me and didn't want to go back to mere pen pal status. Her heart, like mine, was too far-gone.

We would work out any problems in the future. Our tour of New York, seeing Barry someday, spending the rest of our lives together- our dreams were still alive.

Gregory Smith

More then ever, I loved this girl from far across the ocean because she saw me as a whole person- without ever meeting me. I looked forward to our summer of '86 together, like nothing else before.

For the next year we both worked and went to school, saving for tuition and vacation. School kept me from going to Norway, but so did my total lack of independence and the inaccessibility of traveling. We had a long way to go before meeting, but with each day our hearts grew closer.

What would happen if Norway and the United Sates ever went to war? It wasn't a prospect to lose sleep over but we decided to meet halfway, on a deserted island in the middle of the Atlantic Ocean, and let the governments worry about it.

No one was going to stop us now-or so I thought.

I was feeling healthier then ever. No more fractures. Except for the time I took a header out of my chair, reaching down for a box of paints in my bedroom closet. I broke both legs. I was home alone, Mom was at Bingo, my younger brother had moved out to his own apartment by then.

After getting the wheel chair off me I crawled to the phone, calling my brother Mark, who then called the ambulance.

By then Dr. Nicholson had retired. So I went to the local Emergency Room I had my leg casted and then returned home, even beating Mom home. Surprise!

From then on I went to local doctors, but thankfully I didn't need them as often. Once in a while I would have a stress fracture, a lot of aching in my bones when the weather changed from all of the early arthritis I had in my bones. I had so many cracks in my bones; it was hard to tell new fractures from old ones. Many times I didn't even know I had a crack, I was so immune to the pain.

I saw Nicholson for the last time on a sentimental examination, when he wanted to "update" his records. I guess it was closure for him, as he was retiring, and since I was one of his longest-running and rarest, patients I guess he just wanted to say goodbye.

He examined my legs, and I could see the wheels turning in his mind, as he sighed in a low voice, something about the surgeries not working, looking at my bowed, stunted legs, a sense of regret in his hushed tone, as his wife took notes on a yellow pad (She was his semi-secretary too- the first time I ever met Mrs. Nicholson). Meeting her made me see Dr. Nicholson as more then just my longtime physician. He had a life too, beyond the hospital,

I felt more sorry for him then I ever did for myself, knowing he tried so hard to help me for all those years- and he did help me- yet still the ultimate goal, helping me to walk, was never realized.

Still, I thanked him for everything, and reassured him. I was doing well, back in school, trying to make the best of my life. He smiled at me; glad I did not give up.

As a grasp of last hope, both for me and him, he threw out the idea of perhaps going to the famous DuPont Hospital in Delaware for possible "total reconstruction" surgeries- repairing my legs, my back, all of my deformities.

But this time I said no. I was old enough to make up my own mind. There were no guarantees that this "total reconstruction" would work. Maybe I would end up walking, after literally years of rehabilitation. Or maybe I would be a lot worse, bed- bound, unable to sit, let alone stand.

I decided enough was enough. I was more independent then ever; I was going to school and wasn't suffering from fractures anymore. I wasn't giving up-never give up- but I resigned myself to the fact that I could still live and do a lot of good-.even if it meant sitting down rather then standing.

That is how we parted, after so many years, shaking hands. We became a special part of each other's lives. It was like saying goodbye to an old friend. But I was sure we would never forget each other.

I breezed through my first year at the community college, getting straight A's in all of my courses, still surprised at my success. With each success it made me try harder and become even more determined to graduate.

I was feeling better about myself. The 1980's were my coming out party. Even though I couldn't improve my legs I could work on other parts of me. Like my smile. Now that I had more reasons to smile, I wanted my teeth to look nice. O.I. often affects dental health too, making the teeth brittle, and discolored. As I grew braver I wanted to do something about it, and found less resistance from family and friends.

My brother Pat had braces on his teeth, and they turned out great. As always, I looked at myself so much differently then how others looked at me. I dreamed I could have a great smile too. Why not?

So after a long process of getting my teeth filled, cleaned and bleached- I had many years of dental health to catch up on- I was ready for braces- or so I thought.

I wanted to go to the same Orthodontist who treated Pat, but his office had steps to contend with. This was still before the Americans with Disabilities Act was passed, making it a law that buildings, especially new ones, were to be accessible. So I tried another Orthodontist in town. His office was accessible, so I scheduled an appointment.

After the examination, this guy looked at me, wearing a frown and said something like "Braces cost a lot of money. You're in a wheel chair. Do you really need Braces?"

I couldn't believe the prejudice! I think he was afraid to tackle the job, because of my O.I. I guess he was trying to be honest, but I couldn't believe he was saying "You're crippled—why do you want nice teeth?"

Now, I had experienced rudeness in the past. I was even patted on the head, like a dog once in an elevator. But I never faced the ignorance I was encountering now I felt like running over his toes.

After the ADA law was passed, many physical barriers were coming down. There were more ramps, parking places, and cut curbs. Life was a bit easier for someone in a chair, especially compared to the old days when I was a kid, and we literally had to call a restaurant or movie theatre just to check if there were steps to deal with.

Handicapped seating at sporting events and concerts initially left me with mixed feelings. Back in the old days, people in wheelchairs were stuck in corners or in the back of stadiums, arenas, and theatres, paying the same ticket prices as able-bodied folk, yet with no choice of location. If the crowd stood up you couldn't see a thing. It sucked. But with the newer facilities— and newer laws— handicapped seating has improved.

But I always thought it was a strange concept. Realistically, wheelchairs may not be accessible in all locations. That's life. So handicapped seating was beneficial to the disabled.

Yet in another way, who would say, "OK, everyone who is black must sit here. The Chinese need to sit in this section. Anyone different stay with their own kind." Think about it. Put up signs which say "Hispanic Section" or "Deaf Section." Ridiculous!

At first I even bought into this idea. Admitted ashamed and embarrassed, I felt strange sitting next to people who looked and acted differently, some drooling uncontrollably, some yelling out for unknown reasons. I felt like we were all on display, at a circus, and I felt uncomfortable about my feelings. I wanted to be with the "normal" fans, yet I was handicapped too.

Then I woke up. What the hell was I thinking? Who the hell was I? I was handicapped, and should be proud. In fact, I may have been even more handicapped—in my embarrassing attitude—than these brave souls I sat with.

From then on, I felt at home in the handicapped section. I didn't stick out in a crowd and actually had a good time. I made some friends—all ages, all races, all disabilities—even just for the night in those sections. We enjoyed the events together, total strangers, yet linked as one. Most of all, I admired the courage to enjoy life and be as "normal" as anyone. The hell with what others think, ignore the stares. Just enjoy the ballgame or show, enjoy the moment and the friendship around you.

But even though physical barriers were slowly crumbling, the not seen barriers of discrimination remained. I found this out when I visited that Orthodontist. Old views die hard. I went home discouraged, but angry, and no matter how much Mom tried to reassure me that "it's all right", I knew what I wanted, and was determined not to let one jerk deter me.

So I got an appointment with Pats' Orthodontist. My family said they would help me with the steps, if the doctor agreed to treat me. They saw how bad I felt, how self-conscious I was, and didn't want me to fall back into my low self-confidence days.

"Sure, we can do it," Dr. Ginsburg said, after looking at my teeth. I never forgot him, because he gave me a chance. I'm sure my condition was a concern, and he took the time to research O.I. and consult my bone doctors. But at least he was willing to try. He knew how important it was to me, not only to look better and improve my bite, but equally important, to give my self-esteem a boost.

I was thrilled, and didn't mind wearing braces for two-and -a -half years. I endured the pain (what was a little more pain?), the rubber bands, the loss of eating hard or sticky foods (I missed my corn on the cob for several years) the monthly visits to tighten the metal, the rough wires scraping my gums, the struggling up and down the steps. But we did the best we could, and sometimes Dr. Ginsburg would come out to the parking lot as I sat in the front seat of our car, especially when the weather was bad and I couldn't make it up the steps to the office. So he would just check me out or tighten my braces in the car.

In the end all of the sacrifice was worth it. When my braces were finally removed my smile still wasn't like Tom Cruise- Dr. Ginsburg could only do so much with what he had to work with- but the gaps between my teeth were no more, and I was proud to open my mouth and flash those dimples.

Most of all it was a victory over prejudice and a triumph of dignity. I planned on living for a while now, and my smile would last forever.

Bolder chances followed. I grew a moustache to look more mature, and even changed the part in my hair to reflect the current style (what a rebel!).

Every risk was frowned upon. Anything different, not of the norm, was viewed as not fitting into the stereotype of what I "should" be- at least to others.

Breaking the mold was scary, but with each venture came more acceptance, deeper self-esteem, and increased independence to become an individual.

Dating opened up a whole new world to me. I was always self-conscious about my legs, so even though I was meeting more girls in college, I was still afraid to ask any of them out. To my surprise, girls were asking me! I felt bad that I couldn't drive and felt weird about a girl picking me up for a date. But my friends kept encouraging me, Laurie included, by saying, "If a girl likes you enough, she won't mind."

I just had to ask- or had the courage to accept an invitation. Yes, I was surprised how many college girls- younger then me in age- didn't care about my disability. I was limiting myself by not giving myself a chance to have fun.

So once again I bucked society. To most people if you're disabled you're not supposed to have a girlfriend, let alone sex. And if you do, you better date another disabled person.

Good thing I ignored society again. I went out to parties, to movies, and had fun. I still meant what I wrote to Liv. I wanted to meet her so bad. She was special. But I was meeting girls-face to face-and that was making me believe that my chair wasn't an issue. They were real. They were in America. My friends encouraged me to go for it.

My first real girlfriend was named Teresa. Her handle was Silver Fox, and I met her from the CB radio. I found her like magic one night as I was cruising by channel 20. She was talking to some other people, I said hello, and we talked the rest of the evening.

She liked my sense of humor, my personality. She lived nearby, on the other side of Valley Forge Park with her parents. She was nineteen. I was a lot older. It didn't matter to either one of us. She sounded sweet, and flirted a lot that night.

She claimed she was an "interior decorator", and teased me about driving over to check out my house-especially the colors in my bedroom.

Mercy!

I stammered and tried to act cool, wanting to meet her, yet scared to do so. I had been hurt before by girls on the radio who wanted to meet me, and then mysteriously disappeared once they saw my wheel chair.

Somehow, I found it easy to tell Fox about my disability, in the midst of flirting. Interestingly enough, she didn't seem to care. I thought that once Fox met me, satisfying her curiosity, she would just drift away like the others. So I agreed to meet her.

"Over the weekend?" I offered.

"How about tonight?" she suggested.

Gulp. This girl wasted no time. I wasn't used to this.

When Fox came to the door I couldn't believe my eyes. She was beautiful. Long, curly brown hair, big green eyes, tall and very shapely. As though I had died and gone to heaven.

She came back the next night. And the next. And the next.

I had a girlfriend. Not a crush this time, but still, not a feeling of love, certainly different then what I felt for Liv. I couldn't describe it, because I never experienced that feeling before. All I knew was that it was nice and I liked it.

I still thought of Liv. Still felt the same about her. I felt pangs of guilt. My heart and my head were telling me different things again. Yet from the start, although I was having fun, I knew something just wasn't right.

Forget it, my friends advised. Just enjoy. Who knows if Liv has a guy in Norway? You're lucky, having a gorgeous girl like Fox. I was a little confused by all of this sudden attention. All my life people looked at my legs strangely, and here was a girl who looked at them lovingly, and actually cherished my body.

Best of all, Fox and I got along, at least at the start. She was nice but soon we found we didn't have enough in common. She was into dancing, occasional drinking, hanging around a younger crowd. I was more sedate, shy, knowing what I wanted in life, or at least thinking so.

Still, she was far more experienced then I was, in life and other ways. She was fun, and after years of social isolation, I need some fun in my life. My relationship with Fox was a fantasy. My relationship with Liv, though so far away, seemed much more real.

Going out with a girl was new to me. Fox didn't mind tossing my chair in the back seat of her little car, and off we would go. I felt a little embarrassed about my lack of independence, which played a key part in our fate. It was nice to have someone to call in the morning and late at night, and someone to call me. Fox would drop by school during breaks and we would have lunch. We would drive to Valley Forge Park and have lunch or just park- and usually talk. She was unpredictable, and like Wheel chair Willie a few years before, she was bringing me out of my shell. I wasn't spending my Saturday nights at home anymore, at least not alone. I was getting out and doing things, and felt like a "normal" person.

I had led a sheltered life because of my disability, so I really didn't know how to act when it came to going out to dinner or to the movies with a date. But I was learning pretty fast in this whirlwind relationship.

I had never been to a movie with a girl, other then Mom, in twenty years, since I saw "Old Yeller" as a kid. The first movie Fox and I saw together was "Back To The Future" with Michael J. Fox, an appropriate title. To Fox, it was just another date. To me, it was marvelous- the sights, the sounds, being with a crowd of people, on a Friday or Saturday night. So this was how the rest of the world lived!

Fox's parents were nice. They didn't openly discourage the relationship, but they weren't doing cartwheels either. They treated it as though it wouldn't last long, so why get upset? I could sense, after years of experience, when people were being patronizing, not being honest, and I'm sure they were telling her, "What are you doing? You are young, pretty- why are you seeing a guy in a chair?"

I couldn't be the "buddy" most Dads dream about, working on cars together with their daughter's boyfriend, watching sports. Fox's Dad was nice, but didn't really warm up to me, especially when he had to help me up the few steps into their condo. Her Mom was nicer, but I could see it in her eyes, the disapproval. Although Fox told them I was in college, working, and trying to earn my degree, what future did I have with her?

Luckily she didn't listen to them- at first. But her parents still had a lot of influence in her life especially since she still lived at home. She listened to her friends as well, peer pressure.

Her parents were wise people, knowing it wouldn't last long. I wish they 'd warned me too. I guess everyone needs to learn the hard way.

Mom, on the other hand, didn't mind I now had a girlfriend, although she was surprised. I guess my family were getting used to surprises from me- college, working, braces on my teeth, now a girlfriend. She always thought I would turn out to be a priest, so when I expressed what I thought was a normal interest in girls, it caused some raised eyebrows. They were sure I was going to get hurt, sure it wouldn't last. Why was I the only one convinced that it would last?

But end it did. About two months after we met. There were other guys off and on the radio. Maybe that's' why Fox's parents weren't too upset-they knew Fox changed boyfriends frequently. That was Fox, and she was young, and really didn't want to be tied down to one guy. And I guess I couldn't blame her, but why was it me who was going to get hurt?

While Fox wanted to go out with whomever she wanted, I wanted an old-fashioned type of relationship- you know, one girl, one guy. Just like in the movies, the old hopeless romantic I was.

I soon found out she was cheating on me from people on the radio. My heart was broken, but I couldn't say I wasn't warned. Maybe Fox really did care for me, or maybe it was just a fling, an experiment, to date someone "different". I viewed the time together so differently; like I was now "normal", like it was going to last forever, like she really loved me and was devoted to me-only me.

I was angry, bitter and hurt, especially with myself, for letting my heart get crushed. After everything I gave her- and that was part of the problem. I gave her everything I could afford, which wasn't much on my limited budget: flowers, cards, and gifts. I was always there for her, always calling on time, always apologizing for things I didn't need to feel sorry for. I even forgave her when she confessed that one weekend away from me in Maryland, visiting friends, she had a night with a truck driver she talked to on the radio, a guy probably old enough to be her father.

I didn't get much respect or care in return. A relationship is a two-way street, but I was going one-way, down a dead-end street.

I didn't regret giving Fox the cards, the flowers. I spoiled her as I would Liv and every other relationship in the future. That was just me, probably a sense of insecurity, that if I didn't send flowers or a card, maybe the girl would find an excuse to leave? That was too deep, psychologically, to think about back then, but it was probably true.

Fox owned the power in our relationship and she used it to her advantage. She knew she could get away with anything, get a guy on looks alone. She also knew that, without her, I would return to lonely nights. Trouble was, I knew it too, and allowed her to use me for a while, just not to lose her.

I was stuck- between my heart and my head.

I was too dependent on Fox, instead of establishing my own independence. And I was afraid to seek counsel from family and friends. I could hear the "I told you so's", if I ever admitted that I was heartbroken, so I pretended that everything was fine, even when Fox didn't stop by for days at a time. She was just "busy".

We finally called it quits. It was a hard thing to do, but the best thing. I was a wreck, my schoolwork was suffering for it, and I had to do something about it. We had many good times together-partying, shopping, laughter, quiet times, and intimacy. Although she hurt me at the end, I did give her credit because it did take a lot of courage to take a chance on a guy like me. I'm sure she got the stares as well when we went out, she had to hear the "friendly advice" from family and peers, she was willing to do things for me, like driving, handling the wheel chair, that she didn't need the hassle of with other guys.

So I did thank her for the time we had together. First love can be pretty painful. For weeks after we broke up I cried my eyes out. I was back to my old self, going to school, still with friends at college, but it just wasn't the same as having someone special in ones' life. I didn't want to go back to the old me.

With all the arguments and heartache I felt almost relieved to have it end, to move on. But always with first love, you never feel you will move on. You feel its' the end of the world, and in my situation, I felt I would never find love again. My friends tried to encourage me that I had other things in my life, like college, to keep me busy. Don't throw away what you've earned so far, especially on someone who really didn't care.

I made mistakes, but I knew things could be better with someone else, someone who really cared. Until then, I did have a busy, worthwhile life now. I survived without romance before; I could do it again. But now that I had a taste of romance, both the good and the bad, it made me a much wiser person. And despite the ultimate hurt, I wanted to try again…someday. I wasn't going to give up, and crawl back into a cave I didn't regret Fox.

Everything Fox and I did together, I thought of Liv. Would she like the restaurant? Would Liv appreciate the same movie? Liv was on my mind, and in fairness, I suppose that didn't help matters with Fox.

The last straw was in October when I saw Barry in concert at Caesars in Atlantic City. Fox wasn't really a Manilow fan. She thought he was corny, and she was more into the new, younger music. But she went with me anyway, mainly because I didn't want to go alone.

I thought of Liv, as the 11:30 PM. show started. It was 5:30 am in Norway. She would still be sleeping. I wished she were there with me. That was always our goal- to see Barry together.

Barry was great, as usual. He did a lot of songs form his upcoming album in 1985. The next day I wrote Liv a long, twenty-page letter, detailing the entire show. I couldn't wait to tell her about it. I didn't tell her about Fox, again feeling like a traitor, but since the relationship was ending anyway, I decided not to rock the boat, although again, I didn't give her the chance to understand.

Soon I was to learn the difference between a good relationship and a bad one. I learned there was no one else like Liv. Maybe if or when we met, we would both learn differently, but for now, she was special. I grew closer to her, after dating Fox. Even though we were still six thousand miles away I didn't feel as lonely as I had before. From then on, I didn't date anyone but Liv. I went out for fun, as friends, but romance just wasn't in the cards anymore. I felt the wait would sure be worthwhile.

In Norway, Liv felt the same way. She had gone out with guys who didn't exactly live up to advance billing either. Her old flame, the guy she was engaged to for three years, called her for a drink, out of the blue. Then she found out he was married. He told her that his wife didn't understand him- and she told him good night.

So, no matter how hard we looked we didn't find anyone better for each other. We quit looking. We were meant to be together. It was destiny, so why fight it? Instead we felt lucky and blessed.

And all the while, our summer of '86 was growing closer.

Meanwhile Fox was moving to Vermont. She found a new job there, and we met one last time to say goodbye. We promised to write, maybe even call, and I did send her flowers when she wrote me that she had crashed her car soon after arriving in Vermont, and was laid-up in a hospital for a few days. Old habits die hard, as do old feelings.

But realistically, we knew we would probably never see each other again. She would find another guy, get married, have kids and life would go on. But I would always remember our time together, the good and the bad, and end up a better person because of it.

On the same channel as where I first found her, I listening to her fade away down the turnpike on her way to Vermont. When she ended by saying she "loved" me, a twinge, a spark occurred in my heart. But it was on to better things in life, with so much more to do, and more to look forward to, in the months and years just ahead.

5. SOMEWHERE DOWN THE ROAD

In November of 1985 I received the best birthday surprise of all- a phone call from Liv. Overseas calls are expensive, especially for university students with no money, so the call was short but sweet. It was great to hear her voice and even better when she said, "I love you" as we said farewell.

That is when our relationship extended to verbal contact too. I phoned her for Christmas, thanking her for a present- a language book, which promised to teach me to speak Norwegian in only ten minutes a day. I rifted through the flashcards in the book and pasted the tiny stickers around the house, determined to learn a respectable amount of Norwegian to surprise Liv by the following summer.

Those holidays were spent quietly with our families. Liv spent New Year's Eve curled up on her Mom's couch, fighting a cold. As 1986 rang in, and the "Big Apple" dropped in Times Square, I silently wished Liv a Happy New Year. 1985 was great. Writing to her all year was like a splash of sunshine in my life. I knew that '86 would be even better. Meeting Liv was something to look forward to- the summer of our dreams.

I graduated from the community college with a grade point average of 3.95. Not bad. One B over two years. I received a standing ovation at graduation, and also won the Alumni Award, an honor which goes to the student who has achieved, both academically and has overcome adversity, not only during the two years in school, but through out life. I received a plaque for my wall, and a similar plaque was hung in the school's gym, for posterity.

So, I had my Associate's Degree in Human Services, a far cry from where I was just two years earlier- lost, in search of a career, a goal, a direction in my life. I made a lot of friends on the way and converted a lot of doubters into believers- including myself.

But I wasn't ready to stop there. I knew that an Associate's Degree wasn't good enough to get a decent job in the Social Work field. I needed at least a Bachelor's Degree, and that meant two more years of school.

Laurie felt the same way, so we went through the process again, even before graduating from community college. We started looking for a university to transfer to. The question was where- and could we afford it?

Those Are the Breaks

We really couldn't afford not to go for it. Laurie and I were a team, and I was glad to hear that she was willing to go wherever I was going, not only because she was my ride and we loved carpooling together, but because we were friends, and still needed the support we gave each other, and the praise and encouragement no one else could offer.

It was always a dream to attend Saint Joseph's University in Philadelphia. St. Joe's was my favorite Big Five basketball team when I was growing up. Everyone in the Philadelphia area has a favorite Big Five School to root for. My brothers were all different in their favorite teams: Tommy liked Villanova, Pat cheered for LaSalle. Temple and Penn weren't represented. But the Hawks of St. Joseph's were my team, as the Phillies were.

I loved the Hawks because they seemed to always be the underdog, a scrappy team that wasn't afraid to dive for loose balls on the floor or get down and dirty during a game. I could identify with being scrappy. Plus, I thought the Hawk mascot, wings perpetually flapping during a game, was cool.

But when it came time to actually choose a college, St. Joe's was out because it was too far to travel. Everyday. Accessibility as well as transportation was key factors. So was acceptance into the program.

We didn't want to travel into the city, even though our GPA's were good enough to get into most area colleges. We applied to several places, going through the red tape of paperwork again, applying for more grants, more loans, taking entrance exams. Some schools were ruled out automatically because they weren't accessible. Some were ruled out because of travel limitations. The curriculum was also a factor too.

We finally decided on West Chester University, a small school outside of Philadelphia. It was very affordable, an intimate school, easy to get to, easy to cross the campus, the professors very accessible, the classroom sizes small enough to not be overwhelmed. And yet it was still a university, and respected locally for its Social Work program.

The campus was fairly accessible, although the small converted farmhouse on the south end of the campus, where most of the social work classes were held, had a few steps to contend with. Soon that problem was eliminated, as a few students build a portable ramp for me, which would serve for other disabled students down the road.

I remember meeting Mrs. Joyner, then the head of the Social Work Department. She was young, friendly, outgoing. She laughed when I naively asked if my grade point average was "good enough' to consider admission to her program. A 3.95 good enough? Even from a community college? She never let me forget that.

73

Both Laurie and I were accepted at West Chester. We couldn't wait to get started, excited about the upcoming two years, realizing it would be more hard work, even harder then the previous years. This time, we would have to do internships during each year, sort of on the job training programs. We would have to take classes during summers, cramming fifteen weeks of a course into five, wishing we could be on the beach instead of in a hot classroom for four hours each day.

But the thought of the ultimate - that diploma- kept us going. We were determined to enjoy the upcoming summer, but still had our eye on the prize,

With visas all set, I admired Liv's courage as our summer plans began to take shape. Visiting a strange country (and a strange guy), flying so far just to meet me- words couldn't express my love for her.

We planned on visiting New York, Philadelphia, Valley Forge, plus I wanted Liv to share our family activities: a baseball game, the Jersey shore, family summer picnics and barbecues. My family looked forward to meeting her almost as much as I did. Mostly, Liv and I agreed to take this summer to really get to know each other, then take it from there.

It was June 15, the night before Liv's arrival. I called to wish her a safe trip. I would be at the airport to greet her. I spent an anxious, sleepless night, watching the stars outside my bedroom window. In only a matter of hours I would meet Liv.

It took us three hours to drive to Kennedy Airport in New York, (Mom, Aunt Sue and Uncle Henry accompanied me, with Henry braving the traffic, as I rode shotgun in the front seat). The distance was nothing compared to Liv's trip. She was winging over the ocean, her journey close to eight hours.

As I watched the crowds in the overseas terminal, reality was setting in. Fidgety in a suit and tie, I wondered what would happen if we hated each other? This is fun, I told myself. Why worry? I was only going to finally meet the girl of my dreams.

Suddenly all those letters we wrote, how we were matched by the fan club, our first letters seeking a pen pal- everything flashed across my mind as I waited.

I watched as travelers happily and tearfully greeted each other with kisses and hugs. There were many different kinds of people flooding the terminal, different languages being spoken. The enormity of it all hit me, and I grew even more nervous. Luggage seemed to be everywhere. People held up homemade signs to attract their traveling friends.

As Liv's plane landed the butterflies in my stomach were doing their own little three-point landings. My heart skipped a beat each time a blue-eyed blonde female emerged from customs. Still no Liv. Did she miss her flight? I forgot that she needed to pass through customs, since she was flying on a student-fare ticket. Was she at another terminal, searching the airport for us? No, her flight number was there on the board, and the plane had landed.

Just as I was about to go bananas, Liv appeared out of customs. "Is that her?" Mom asked. The smile on Liv's face when she spotted me was the answer.

She carried one large suitcase and a shoulder bag. She looked the same as in her photo- beautiful, dressed in a summer white outfit. Sleeveless top and slacks.

"Hi," she said sweetly, politely shaking hands. After introductions to my family we just took a moment to gaze at each other, eyes finally meeting, and smiled. Nearly two years after becoming pen pals, after all the letters, cards and calls, after missing each other so many times, here we were, face to face, a dream come true.

As Liv helped Henry load her suitcase in the car trunk, Aunt Sue looked at me and said, "She's cute!" I agreed, blushing.

The ride home was full of quiet shyness. Uncle Henry kept things lively, as usual, telling his fishing stories. I had to glance into the backseat several times just to make sure she was really there, and that it wasn't all just a beautiful dream.

It was late, around midnight, when we got home. Liv invited me into the guestroom to talk while she unpacked. It was our first time alone. We looked at each other, Liv sitting on the edge of the bed, with clothes, film and other travel items scattered around the room. A warm breeze blew in the window, the sweet scent of spring flowers filling the room. No longer were we apart to look at those same stars we had searched for so many times in the past.

"It's so good to see you," she whispered.

"It's good to have you here," I softly replied. "Are you…disappointed?"

"No way," she answered, giving me a hug. She was so soft, the scent of her warm body so sweet, the touch I dreamed about for so long. "Anything else you want to know?"

"Yeah, " I said, picking up the hot pink swimsuit on the bed. "When are you going to wear this?"

We laughed, hugging again. Touching was something we

75

dreamed of for so long. Now we held each other for what seemed like a beautiful eternity. It sure beat writing letters.

Our love survived time and distance, and now we were together for a fantastic summer. We would think about August, and having to say goodbye, later. Now we would just try to make every moment count. From that night on we would always be together, even when we were apart.

After getting over her jet lag, Liv and I did some sightseeing, but hanging around the house was fun too. We cuddled on my bed, watching television. Liv's favorites were "Wheel of Fortune" and our crazy American commercials. I showed her beautiful Phoenixville, and we sat in the cool shade of Reeves Park, watching children in the playground, wondering if our kids would someday play there, wondering what our future would hold.

Our first evening alone I gave Liv a little gift I had been saving for so long. It was an emerald necklace, her birthstone.

"You're crazy," she teased, blushing as she kissed me.

It was a perfect, romantic evening, one I had dreamed of forever. Our hearts said one thing, our minds another. Our hearts won.

Holding Liv was unlike anything I had ever felt before. The entire summer felt so right. I came home from my summer job at the nursing home, always bringing Liv a surprise, be it a red rose or M&Ms. She greeted me at the end of each day and we would walk home together (actually, she would push my chair), talking about our day and planning for the evening ahead. We talked about Norway and my visit someday. Then she would hop on the back of my chair (or better yet, my lap), and we would ride into the sunset together, living happily ever after.

Our fantasy.

There were special memories to cherish. Like coming home from the local movie theatre, the Colonial Theatre, in the summer moonlight. One night a stray kitten followed us home before Liv carried it back to the previous block. We laughed at the thought of almost becoming adopted parents.

We suddenly stopped, the night so still, and Liv leaned over the back of my chair and we kissed in the summer darkness, only the crickets and nearby fireflies as witnesses. We began to realize that August would be here too soon.

There were more memories: a warm, sunny day touring historic Valley Forge Park; picnicking among the rolling green hills of the park; Liv learning the delights of a Phillies game; a cheese steak and Philly soft pretzels; the muggy thunderstorm we were drenched in while waiting to see the Liberty Bell outside of Independence Hall; the day we toured the Philadelphia Zoo, Liv taking pictures of me and the other animals,

At night we would cuddle and watch old black and white movies, sharing a Hershey Kiss or two (as well as the even sweeter kind). We loved to sit outside on the front porch amidst the cool breeze, especially after a shower, watching the twinkling stars peek out of the dark sky as the sunset painted the west in flaming colors. Many nights we had gazed at those same stars alone, thinking of each other, so far away. Now it was unbelievable that we could watch the sunset, now so close.

The best times were spent together in my room, the lights low, with Manilow music playing softly in the background, whispering dreams, listening to heartbeats, a train whistle in the distance or a rumble of thunder on the horizon. I loved those nights, with the scent of lilacs from the garden smelling almost as sweet and fresh as Liv.

Again, I couldn't believe, after years of rejection and stares, that someone so beautiful, could love me- mind, body and soul. It was different then with Fox. I knew Liv loved me- for me.

Those were special times, times I never wanted to end, when "I love you" meant so much. As the summer faded away we knew that somehow, someway we had to be together- always. Life wouldn't be as perfect as that summer. Finishing school and finding real jobs were harsh realities in the future. A lot of hard work and sacrifice to survive the separation again. Time was the true test. If it were meant to be, it would be.

"We'll work something out, love," Liv encouraged. In my heart I knew we could.

Tanning in the yard (the pink swimsuit was worth the wait), meeting other Manilow fans, browsing through the mall, buying eight Manilow albums at a time (the ones she couldn't find in Norway), and getting strange looks from the heavy metal record clerk, a cozy dinner for two, discovering popcorn at the movies (no popcorn in Norwegian theatres). All wonderful memories. But the best was yet to come- our long awaited trip to New York.

The highlight was strolling around the Statue of Liberty together, the towering Manhattan skyline across the sparkling bay. We kissed, watching the small boats dotting the windy harbor. We were in a world of our own; until my family finally caught up with us on the next ferryboat. Still, it was the hallmark of a wonderful, romantic summer.

Liv was one of the family already. She was still introduced as "pen pal", although hints of romance were evident. I'm sure no one thought this fling would really last, especially after the summer was over and even I had to admit that I worried that I may never see Liv again.

For a week before her departure I cried, sneaking into the bathroom. A few times she noticed my misty eyes, and she would hug me, saying, "Be happy, for me!" Yet I could see the sadness and uncertainty in her eyes as well.

Liv finished packing away our summer memories, and I remembered that first night when she arrived, two months earlier. How the summer had so swiftly passed.

My family stopped by, bearing gifts, biding their farewells, Liv hugging the little ones and promising to return. I could only try to smile, keeping everything inside.

We cuddled for the last time in my room, reliving our moments together, laughing and sighing over our memories. It wasn't fair, other people in love, hand-in-hand wherever we went that summer- yet knowing that we couldn't be together- just yet. Somehow we were determined to beat the odds. The future was exciting yet cloudy. Marriage? Visas? Jobs? Where would we live? Our families and friends- how would they respond? So many things to consider.

We planned on meeting again next summer, taking it one day at a time, and promising never to give up on each other. We sealed it with a kiss as a surprise song played on the radio. "Somewhere Down The Road" was a Manilow song about two people separated by fate, yet destined to meet again. Nothing could be more appropriate, or more special.

"...And that was for Liv-Karin, love always from Greg. Thanks for a great summer..."

We sat in the airport; summer over, proud that we really met, knowing now there was nothing we couldn't do together. But next summer seemed so far away.

Time to board the plane. An airline employee offered to take me aboard first, thinking I had a ticket. Wishful thinking.

Liv hugged Mom, then me for the final time, tears in our eyes. "I'll write back first," she promised. "Thanks for everything. Love you!"

I wished I could hold her forever. In an instant she was gone, and suddenly I felt very lonely.

We watched the jet soar overhead; it's red tail a blur in the distance. Away went my heart, disappearing before my eyes.

Liv cried across the ocean. Oslo was cold and rainy when she arrived there, the weather as dreary as her mood. The flowers I had sent ahead to her apartment helped brighten her, a reminder that I wasn't about to forget her, despite the distance between us once more.

The remainder of the summer was spent missing Liv. I couldn't sleep or eat, passing the silent, dark guestroom, crying.

Even though it was nice to be home again, Liv was missing me too. Showing pictures and souvenirs to family and friends was exciting. But late at night, when all was quiet, she remembered our goodnight kiss and her heart felt empty again.

It was strange being pen pals again. Her letters reminded me how far apart we were once more. It helped when she wrote that she still loved me, now more then ever, and we would build on our love, not tear it apart. Listening to "Somewhere Down The Road" would be hard for a while, but it was a warm memory of days to come.

Already we were counting the days until our next meeting. An international romance isn't easy, but it isn't impossible, if the love and trust is strong enough. We were far from giving up.

Liv sent photos of our summer together. There was the zoo again, the Phillies game, New York City. It wasn't just a dream. Seeing her again kept me going through the upcoming long winter days and nights.

With my Associate's Degree proudly displayed on my wall I took a deep breath and continued on. The new school year would bring exciting challenges but life would be boring otherwise. New faces, new classes. Another year of scraping for student loans, studying hard, working crazy hours, bouts with illness and loneliness. Thoughts of Liv kept me pushing hard.

Now, I had the feeling that nothing could stop me. The Bachelor's Degree was mine to reach out for- and hold.

A few things stood out during my two years at West Chester. I joined a Disabled Activist group on campus, and we helped to make the university more accessible. It helped me to learn I could help myself while still helping others. I also had two internships during my final two years.

My Junior Practicum I did at the Manor. It was great working there, this time in a shirt and tie, counseling the residents I had grown to love. I worked with a great social worker named Eileen, who was Director of Social Services at the time. She was very pretty too, which made life easier. Most of all, she taught me about social work, yet she never forgot that I was a student, bound to make mistakes. Even later in my career, as I became a seasoned social worker I was still learning something new each day.

Eileen was always smiling and laughing, .She had such a positive attitude, which I never forgot. Although I couldn't do much of the documents, since officially I still wasn't a social worker, I did a lot of small things around the office- copying, filing, and stuffing envelopes. But mostly I was learning the ropes about what it took to be a social worker in a nursing home setting. I attended the meetings, became disciplined in my hours, and learned the ins and outs of the job, which would prove invaluable down the road.

I worked three days a week, and attended classes as well. Ironically, I would eventually supervise two students from West Chester when I became a social worker. It was great giving back, and I remembered my days as a learning student. I loved the work, and really wanted to experience everything I could. I found that nursing home social work was my niche.

I would counsel residents mostly, and help families too. I learned how hard the doctors and nurses worked, how the business office and administration worked behind the scenes. It was far different then when I worked there as a volunteer. It was like a totally different world, and it gave me a better appreciation of what it was like to run a nursing home.

The residents were very comfortable with me, since they knew me already from my volunteer days. They trusted me, since they knew I had been in the same boat in my past, first as a patient, someone disabled, a person in need.

I'm not saying that one needs to be disabled to help others in need, but it helps because I could emphasize with the residents.

I will never forget Eileen's final piece of advice on my last day of the practicum. I thought she was going to give me some really long, deep theory, but her advice was very simple, and surprising.

"Don't ever lose your sense of humor," she simply stated. "You'll need it."

How right she would be! No matter the situation- facing illness, death on a daily basis, there was always room to smile, to make others happy, and to keep one's sanity. No matter what, life would go on, the sun would rise the next day, and it wasn't worth stressing out about. They told us in college- a typical social worker might only last four years in the field before burning out. The work was so emotionally draining, you had to be strong- and keep that sense of humor- to survive.

Those Are the Breaks

My Senior Practicum was spent at the local hospital. How ironic was that! Born there, the place where my O.I. first surfaced, and here I was, a social worker.

My supervisor this time was Jean, an older lady with silver hair, who had twenty years of experience in the field. She was retiring that year, and I was to be her last student. She didn't have a degree-guess a degree wasn't needed back in the old days- but her knowledge was tremendous. She knew all the resources in the area, knew phone numbers by heart. She oozed common sense, which was a lot of what social work is all about. I learned that what I was learning in the classroom was important- the different theories and such. But until I got out there and actually did it- using basic common sense and sensitivity- along with my education- social work was a piece of cake.

Social Work in a hospital was a lot different then in a nursing home. Different population, different age groups, different kinds of cases. It was great experience and helped me to develop my skills and grow as a person. I would work on the floors one day, counseling patients and families, or maybe one day working in the Emergency Room. That was probably the toughest part of the job, often consoling loved ones when a family came into the ER after an accident.

My very first case in the hospital was counseling a young girl who had tried to commit suicide. She was only fourteen, and had swallowed ninety-two aspirin. Luckily they found her in her bedroom, rushed her to the hospital, pumped her stomach, and saved her life. Now it was my job to find out why she did it.

Entering the room I was scared to death. The pretty girl with the long blonde hair looked at me suspiciously. She asked who I was. I replied a social worker, here to talk. She groaned, "Oh, you're only a social worker. I thought you were a Psychiatrist."

Only a social worker? I felt so low. It was even worse when she found out that I was "just a student" too. But I admitted that I was scared too, and I think my honesty made her feel comfortable-maybe even sorry- for me, and she opened up a bit. We had some common ground. We were both scared and needed a friend.

We talked and eventually I got out of her that she had overdosed because of a forbidden romance. Her next-door neighbor was twice her age. She would visit him "to do homework and watch television", but when her parents forbade her to see him anymore, she took the pills.

I convinced her that life was worth living, and she was lucky to be alive. I couldn't fix her romance problems, because she really didn't want to hear my advice anyway, so I just listened, mostly because I was afraid, and really, wasn't sure what advice to offer. But I found that listening was good enough. She needed someone to talk to. Her parents wouldn't listen, her friends didn't understand.

I didn't do anything heroic or special, as in most of my future cases. I just listened and cared. I listened intently, not casually, and this skill earned her trust and would be a very valuable skill in the future. It was more then a skill- it was just I, being myself, not afraid to take off the mask of "social worker" and allow myself to just be a caring person who was willing to help.

In the end, I offered a referral of counseling for the pretty blonde and her parents once she was discharged. It was up to them to follow through with the help. Her parents eyed me cautiously as well. Who was I, a student, and disabled no less, telling them what they should do?

I never forgot her name, since she was officially my first case in the hospital, and several years later I was happy to see her name listed as one of those who graduated from a local high school. I felt, in some small way, I helped her reach that point. I was glad she decided not to give up.

I worked with alcoholics, the homeless, people with insurance problems, arranged discharge care, you name it. It was great experience. Although I still loved nursing home social work, the knowledge I obtained at the hospital for those nine months would serve me well as time went on.

I was breezing though most of my classes at West Chester, especially my social work and psychology courses. They were most important to my career, so I was glad I was doing so well.

But there were two required courses I needed to take- and pass- in order to graduate, Spanish and Math. I dreaded both.

Actually, I wanted to take sign language as my language requirement. I thought that sign would come in handy in my profession (and indeed, there were times I could've used sign language down the road). If I wanted to work with the elderly, I realized some might be deaf, some hard of hearing, so I really wanted to learn sign.

Unfortunately, the classes were only offered in Philly. Laurie didn't want to drive into the city twice a week, so we decided to take Spanish instead.

I studied Spanish in high school, although I forgot a lot of it over the years. If you don't use it, you lose it. But at least I knew the basics, so Spanish it was.

Spanish I was a stroll in the park, learning simple words and phrases. Spanish II would be harder, learning different tenses. Spanish II was offered during the summer. Fifteen weeks worth of Spanish crammed into five weeks. I wanted to graduate on time, so both Laurie and I signed up for the summer course .It was a sizzling summer, but I still looked like a ghost. I didn't have time for a vacation or lying out in the backyard.

We were there, five days a week, every morning for four hours. The professor was really cool, a short, chubby guy with a beard. A colorful character, literally. He looked exactly like Pancho Villa, and he often strolled into class wearing Bermuda shorts, red socks and a brightly colored flowered shirt. He told us the first day "Look, I don't want to be here as much as you don't want to be here. We all would rather be on the beach. But we are here, so let's make the best of it."

It was hard work, with a test each Friday. Sink or swim. Learn it fast or don't- no in-between. Luckily the professor kept things lively and fun. So it wasn't such a burden to attend class each day, while the rest of the world was on vacation.

That was my life for five weeks: go to class, come home and work [part-time, study at night, then back at the same routine the next day. I only had Spanish to study, so I ate, drank and slept Spanish.

If I stopped and thought about the frantic pace of the course, I never would have gotten through it. So I didn't stop and think. I just did it.

People dropped out of the class, and I imagined them soaking up the sun while I was sweating it out in class each day.

I thought of Liv and wanted to spend my summer with her. I really wanted to fly to Norway, meet her family and friends, see all those sights in Oslo and Larvik she had told me about. But school kept me anchored to home, so my trip was put on hold again.

I ended up with an A. Spanish III loomed ahead in the next semester. Everyone told horror stories of Spanish III. I needed to pass it to graduate. I got through the first two Spanish courses- how hard could the final one be?

Spanish III turned out to be a nightmare. First, the lessons were much harder. We were speaking only in Spanish in class. We were writing only in Spanish. One of the tests was writing an essay, difficult in itself- in Spanish. Different tenses, more elaborate words and phrases.

Spanish Lab, which we attended once a week, was the toughest part of the course. I didn't have trouble reading or writing the language. But I couldn't seem to catch it- hearing the words. The language tended to be spoken rather quickly, so listening to Spanish in Lab, and trying to decipher words, answer questions, and make sense of it all was a challenge. I wanted to say "Slow down!" but it sure made us learn the language-or else.

    To make matters worse, the professor was a real nutcase, a far cry from Pancho Villa last summer. Tall, rail-thin, with bad spiked hair and an equally bad goatee, he was a tyrant in class. Screaming, ranting and raving, he laid down the law the first day of class. He demanded perfection and wouldn't tolerate anything less. He wasn't above ridicule, and often brought the female students to tears by calling them "stupid" or making fun of their answers. He was a real drill sergeant. He put up with no nonsense and no excuses. You really had to earn your grade in his class.

    One day he walked into class with a large yardstick, cracking it against his desk and threatening to use it, if we didn't study or answer his questions correctly. He didn't treat us like adults, more like children. Everyone dreaded this guy, and when other students found out we had this particular professor's class, they asked why in the world did we take it?

    In our situation, it was the only Spanish III class that would fit our schedule. Plus it was a challenge. We did hear negative rumors about Professor Evil, but how bad could he really be?

    Soon, the faint-hearted dropped out of class within the first week. From a class of about thirty maybe only twelve of us die-hards- or more like idiots- stayed. Some had no choice.

    Professor Evil tended to hit on the good-looking girls in class. I could easily imagine, if they didn't cooperate- accepting his personal tutoring out of class- he could make life hell for that hour several days a week when we did get together.

    He was psychotic, and no one had the nerve to challenge him, or report him to higher authorities on campus. We just took the abuse, and he lightened up a bit as he weeded out the survivors. Still, even to the end, he kept up the rough exterior.

    In one way, it made everyone study hard-or else. He knew he had the power, and didn't hesitate to use it. In another way, his pacing the classroom made everyone on edge. Just never knew where he would stop, the desk he would hover over and challenge with a question.

    He kind of liked me. He called me "Smith", and didn't treat me that much differently then anyone else, but at least he didn't ridicule me. Maybe he knew that ridicule either wouldn't bother me- or may break me, judging from my appearance.

    I was doing surprisingly well, especially considering my struggles in Spanish Lab, but I was really getting into it, even watching Spanish cable channels on television. I constantly reviewed notes and flashcards.

It got so bad I sometimes forgot myself and wrote out birthday cards in Spanish by mistake. I was brainwashed.

I wanted to do the best I could, as in any class, but in another way, I wanted to prove to this jerk that I wasn't a quitter- as the rest of the group was determined to do. Pretty soon we bonded as a group and it became a "we versus Professor Evil" thing. We hated Professor Evil for making our lives miserable, but he did make us work and learn. Why did discipline have to be so hard?

At the end of the semester was the big final exam. It covered the entire four months. A make or break test. I had a solid B so far, so unless I totally bombed the final, I was hoping I would at least pass. Most of all, the class was relieved that, after taking the final exam- Professor Evil would become a memory.

When we entered the classroom for the test at 9:00 that morning, it was dead silence, like entering the gas chamber. Everyone tried to stay positive and encourage each other, but deep down inside we were all scared to death. It was only one class. It wasn't life or death. Life would go on, we would all graduate, and live happily ever after.

But for most of the students who were teetering on failing the course, this final exam meant either pushing back graduations-as we were all seniors- or even worse, having to repeat the course, maybe with Professor Evil himself in charge.

After we got settled in, and Professor Evil walked into the room, somber, dressed all in black as always, it was like a miracle had occurred.

He actually broke into a wide grin, and before the test started, he offered everyone doughnuts and coffee, encouraging us to help ourselves. He was like a different guy. The tension eased. We shook our heads in disbelief.

He had softened near the end of the semester. It was a combination of things: sickness in the class, a student involved in a car accident, and the fact that we were twenty of the most hard- working, honest students that were ever assembled in one group.

Plus it didn't hurt when the class took Professor Evil out to lunch one afternoon. We went to a Mexican restaurant (as close to Spanish as we could get), ordered everything in Spanish, got a few drinks in to the professor, and he loosened up quite a bit, even calling us by our first names instead of our last names for a change.

The final wasn't so bad, maybe because the answers came easy. After studying so hard, after learning the language inside and out, we couldn't help but recall the answers.

Then it hit me. Professor Evil's tactics ultimately worked. I saw him in a new light. The hard work paid off. Sure, he didn't have to be so psychotic, but he did make us learn- and that was the main objective of our four months together. He made sure we wouldn't forget Spanish- or him.

As we each finished the exam, we exited, and there he was, waiting for each student outside in the hall. He shook my hand, smiling, and said what a pleasure it was having me in his class. I actually thanked him, for not playing favorites because of my disability, for pushing me just as hard.

"I wasn't the best student," I admitted to him, "but I tried hard." That pretty much summed up my entire college experience.

"I know you did," he said, actually smiling. He was human after all. He wanted me never to forget him (how could I?), and be sure to stop by and say hello if I was ever on campus after graduation.

Yeah, right!

But Professor Evil showed himself to be a pussycat after all. I earned- and I use that word strongly- earned a B in the course. Most of all, I survived the challenge, maybe the toughest class of my college career.

Laurie and I let out a yell as we left the building, like we had conquered Mount Everest. We watched the other students slowly filter by, waving so long, wishing them a nice vacation; good luck and Merry Christmas Laurie had a relaxing smoke, as if she just had sex.

But there would be one final challenge looming ahead in the last semester, my final semester before graduation. The big, ugly monster, which stood in front of that diploma and me, had a very small name- Math.

Yes, my worst nightmare in school was summed up in that four-letter word: Math.

I hate Math. It went all the way back to my days at Penn. Any kind of Math was horrifying, even simple stuff like fractions. In order to earn my degree, get a good job, become more independent, and eventually marry Liv, I had to pass Math. It was a required course. It was only my entire future, which rested with this course.

I picked the most basic Math course, skipping Physics, Geometry, Algebra, and all of those fancy courses. I just wanted to pass, earn my three credits and go on with life, as we know it. Different then other courses, where I wanted to do my absolute best. In Math, I just wanted to survive.

Those Are the Breaks

I bought a new pocket calculator, sharpened my pencils and went to work. Our professor was an older guy with frizzy white hair, Einstein's brother, perhaps. He promptly informed the class on the first day that most of his students failed his courses. He even listed a detailed chart on the blackboard, showing the grades from his classes over the last five years. There was a heavy slant towards the "F" column. Was there a place reserved in that category for me too?

Whereas Professor Evil from Spanish was overly emotional- on the crazy side- this guy was like a robot. Everything was chart, logical, no emotions, and no feelings.

With such confidence to spur me on, I never worked so hard at anything in my life. Math drove me up the wall. My other courses were challenging too, but Math was the albatross around my neck.

At first class was actually fun. Einstein often brought in dice to help illustrate some of his points. If not Math, then at least I was improving in Craps.

I did well in the first exam until we began studying Statistics, then everything went downhill fast.

I would study hard, then go blank while I was taking the exam. Even though I knew the formulas, I froze. It was like watching life pass before my eyes.

It was all so stupid. Why couldn't I get this? Why did I need to? I know it was a required course. I needed Math to become a better-rounded person, even though becoming a social worker was often a reason to avoid Math in life. Maybe I was trying too hard, and in the process, giving myself anxiety?

Meanwhile, Liv was having her own problems with school. She vowed never to become a tax lawyer. Taxes to her were like fractions to me. She had mountains of reading to do. Her average final exam lasted nearly four hours. And she had five final exams.

Liv was also having trouble with her student loan again. With no student loan, continuing through law school would be difficult. With no student loan, our next summer meeting would be in jeopardy.

Even worse news was the results of Liv's annual medical check-up. Several small cysts were found on her ovaries. They probably weren't serious or else they would have removed them immediately. She told me not to worry. Instead, the doctors asked her to come back in a few months. If the cysts had grown, then they would run tests and decide what to do.

The date of her next check-up was June 16- exactly one year to

87

the day when we first met.

So between Liv's health and Math, I had a lot on my mind that semester I did so much praying-and worrying-during the spring of 1987.

Liv remained cool as always, and I admired her courage. She had to be going through some pretty anxious moments, but that didn't stop her from always encouraging me.

"You can do it, love!" she wrote. "Don't give up. Go in there and pass that exam!"

Liv's health came first. Our next meeting would have to be delayed, especially if she needed to be hospitalized. The only thing I cared about was Liv getting well. It was all that mattered, and made Math seem so unimportant in the scheme of things.

I was holding a low "C" in Math. I wanted to avoid flunking the final and having to repeat the course. That would be like someone shooting himself in the foot-twice.

I couldn't afford to go blank on this final. I had to pass this one. So much was riding on it.

I again ate, drank and slept Math for four solid months. My other paltry exam scores were past history. This was a brand new ballgame. This one was for Liv.

I prayed for strength. I thought of my parents. Of Liv, and I couldn't let them down. I couldn't let myself down. So I went into that exam fighting mad. I wasn't going to let a bunch of numbers ruin my future and my nerves. It was the last exam of my junior year. I worked too hard to let it all slip away now.

Laurie was having similar difficulties. She was in danger of also failing the class as well, so this exam meant much to her too. Let's face it-we were both feelings people, not logical people. That is why we were in social work.

I hid my anxiety by trying to encourage her in the car, the pep talk really intended for both of us. I sounded so confident, I think I fooled myself into believing I could actually pass the upcoming exam.

It was 8:00am. I was nervous as the test began, almost going blank again, the sweat running down my face. Numbers swirled in my head. I closed my eyes, took a few deep breaths, and continued on.

Afterwards, I wasn't sure if I had passed or not. But win, lose or draw, it was over. That in itself was like a ton of weigh off my shoulders.

Waiting for the results was tough. I was never so happy to earn a

"C" in all my life, but when I saw the grades posted, I wanted to do wheelies all over the campus. It was the lowest grade I ever received in college, but I was never more joyous. I passed the biggest barrier between my degree and me. There was still hope that I would be a social worker yet.

Meanwhile, Laurie was delirious with her "d-minus". She was a people person like me, not a rocket scientist. She was on her way too.

The big spenders we were on our tight budgets, we celebrated by going out for pizza. After all, you only live once.

My High School Graduation - 1975

Me and Mom

"Uncle" Henry and "Aunt" Sue Szczesny
taken on front porch at nephew Jimmy's (Easton, Maryland)
June, 1985

CB'ERS AID 'CHINA BOY' - Gregory Smith, 20-year-old son of James and Ann Smith, of 9 Hall St., Phoenixville, was presented with a gift of a Citizen Band radio console sending and receiving set by members of area CB groups. At the presentation at his home, Greg is surrounded by his parents, directly behind him, and by enthusiastic CB'ers. In photo (not in left to right sequence) CB members and call names include, Ray Zeleski, "Ball Joints"; Betty Zeleski, "Lady Stargazer"; Diane Zeleski, "Blue Eyes"; Rich Mince, "Hot Streak"; Kathy Mince, "Sophisticated Lady"; Bill Speacht, "Wolfman"; Bob Fontaine, "Cookie Munster"; Wes Hammerschmidt, "Whiskey"; Harriet Frederick, "Blue Velvet"; Bud Frederick, "Mr. Woodchuck"; Ed Powers, "Daddy Long Legs"; Ron Torjs, "Pecos Bill"; Joanne Lit, "Model A"; and Cecilia Llewellyn, "Weeping Willow."

(Times Herald Photo)

6. COULD IT BE MAGIC

Between school and work I was due for a little fun. In October of 1987 I had an experience, which would last forever.

Barry had written a book. It was called "Sweet Life: Adventures On The Way To Paradise". I bought the first two copies of the autobiography from my local bookstore. I read it that night, cover to cover, in six hours. The other copy I sent to Liv.

The book was great, tracing Barry as a kid growing up in Brooklyn, New York, straight through his superstardom in music.

A promotional book tour was being planned in key cities across the country, with autograph signings at bookstores. The first such stop, as I learned from the fan club, would be at Cherry Hill, New Jersey, right across the river from Philadelphia.

Other then the Hotline announcement (the Hotline was a weekly taped message over the phone from the fan club), the only other publicity was a tiny notice in the book section of the Sunday paper, announcing Barry's appearance at the bookstore at 12:30 PM the following day.

Vicki and Chris were an engaged couple from Philly I had met through the fan club. Actually, Vicki had her own local club. They soon became close friends, and were just like Wheelchair Willie in my life-friends, a source of fun, and a way for me to become more independent.

They planned on camping out over night in the parking lot of the mall in order to save a spot in line to meet Barry. They asked me to join them.

It was a crazy idea. My good common sense told me no, don't do it .It was a teenager's scheme, and I was older and wiser now. Then the daredevil in me took over, the part Willie and Laurie had always encouraged me to fulfill. "You only live once, "Willie advised. "Because when you're dead, you're dead a hell of a long time".

In other words, go for it! I may never get the chance to meet Barry Manilow again. I never camped-out before, so it would be an adventure at the very least.

I let Laurie know I was cutting classes the next day, which she was pleased about. Much to Mom's horror I decided to go. Bundled up, with new book in hand. There I was in Vicki's old station wagon, trekking to Jersey on that chilly Sunday night in October.

Mom acted as though I was leaving for boot camp. I assured her that I would call later that evening, and that I would be safe and warm in the car, not to worry. Little good that did, since I didn't know what to expect myself. It may have reassured Mom, but not me.

Vicki and Chris were always great, so Mom wasn't as worried as she might have been. They were a bit wacko concerning Barry, real die-hard fans; so I knew that whatever happened would be fun.

We arrived at the mall around 7:00 PM. The night was already crisp in the autumn air. Our original plan was to sit the cozy, heated car all night, and then take our place in line early the next morning. Then we saw the other campers, fans equally as crazy.

There we were, parked near the bookstore. We noticed the giant posters of Barry's book in the front window, with the sign "Appearing on October 12-Barry Manilow". The line, to our delight, was empty.

There were several cars in the lot. We could vaguely make out the passengers, huddled in warm coats. They had to be Manilow fans, as crazy as we were, to be parking in a closed shopping mall on a Sunday evening.

Vicki declared that for once, she was determined to be near the head of the line. She had always been beat out for top honors by members of the dreaded Quarter Noters, a rival area fan club. Not this time!

So, even though Vicki had a bad cold, we unpacked our gear: sleeping bags, food, radio, books, and whatever other provisions we could carry, taking our place beside the bookstore door.

Little by little, other fans joined our line. Next to us was a middle-aged woman, blonde and heavy-set. Her husband thought she was nuts to be out there. But like the rest of us, she was determined to meet Barry. Her daughter would have joined her if it were Madonna.

The line grew, as the evening got colder. Fans from as far away as Cleveland, Ohio arrived by van, as did a bunch from Massachusetts. All in all, about twenty of us brave and hearty souls spent the entire night in line.

Mostly we talked, getting to know each other, sharing Manilow stories. It was like my video party when Liv was in the States, only bigger and without videos. But we did have our cassette players working overtime, playing nothing but Manilow music all night long. We swapped tapes, photos and addresses.

Some people played cards. Most were too cold to do much of anything but shiver or move around, trying to keep warm. The temperature was expected to drop into the high 30's but it seemed colder then that. Many fans headed for their cars occasionally to warm up.

Some sat on lawn chairs, while others sat on the sidewalk with blankets. We had a little overhang above us, outside the mall. It would have provided protection in case of rain but the night was crystal clear, with a bright harvest moon looming above.

Manilow fans tend to be very outgoing, sociable and friendly, and this crowd was no different. It's funny how a group of complete strangers can get to know each other so well after so short a time. Spending the night together can do that to people.

A husband and wife team had the right idea, only emerging from their car every so often to let us know they were still alive. We saved their place in line. By now, the group had started a list to keep the line in order, and to allow people to leave and get something to eat. The all-night doughnut shop was the favorite place to go, not because of the food. It was close by, and the bathroom was accessible, so there was a steady stream of "customers" that night.

Sherry, a fan from Jersey, stopped by in her red sports car. She was a lyricist, looking for her big break into show business. She was also a veteran of camp-outs, and she offered her help if anyone needed anything.

She only lived a few minutes away but she stopped by all night with supplies. She had a warm apartment nearby yet she remained out in the cold, enjoying the event. That was why most of us were out there, freezing- it was the "event" of being there, and something we could look back on over the years.

Around ten o'clock a woman dropped by, claiming to be the manager of the bookstore. She wanted to checkout the crowd, bragging that she knew Barry for years. She also brought some distressing news: the fans wouldn't be able to talk to Barry. A representative from the publishing company would take the book, hand them to Barry for signing, hand them back, and away we would go.

We knew there would be hundreds of fans swarming the bookstore by the following afternoon. We also knew that with so many people, we couldn't expect to hold a long conversation with Barry. But we did expect to get close enough to shake his hand and say hello. After all, that was what we were staying out in line all night for.

We didn't believe the reports, and we protested. Barry didn't treat his fans that way, to be pushed around like brooms.

Before the troublemaker left, she said she would see what she could do to change the situation since she personally knew Barry.

True or not, none of us were going to leave our places now. We were bound to stick it out.

Our faith was rewarded around eleven o'clock when we saw a car slowly pull into the parking lot. It wasn't the police again, who were patrolling the area during the night. They had to think we were harmless-clueless but harmless, only twenty lunatics out there, waiting to meet some singer. The cops didn't return after checking us out.

The car cruised by our line, and we noticed it was a taxi. Now, why would a taxi come through the parking lot on a Sunday evening with the mall closed?

Something was up. Vicki sat up beside my wheel chair, peering at the cab. Chris, already stuffed in his sleeping bag next to Vicki, reached for his glasses.

There were two people in the backseat of the cab, a man and a woman, but we couldn't make out their faces, which were hidden in the shadows. Someone mumbled aloud, "What's going on?" and I made the mistake of wondering, jokingly, "Maybe it's Barry?"

Whoops.

"BARRY!" As soon as the group began to collectively rise, the cab sped off through the lot, turning onto the main road.

"Let's follow them!" Sherry shouted. Vicki, miraculously cured of her cold, jumped into Sherry's car and they took off.

Meanwhile, the rest of us milled around, speculating whom may have been in the cab and why they were so interested in us.

Several tension-filled minutes later, Sherry and Vicki returned, speeding through the lot, horn blaring. They sprang out of the car, shouting at the top of their lungs. We thought they had both lost their minds.

Finally calm enough to speak, Vicki excitedly told the story as the group gathered, panting as she talked a mile a minute.

They had followed the cab to the doughnut shop, where Marc, Barry's personal assistant, and a woman companion emerged. Before Vicki and Sherry returned, Marc was coming out of the shop with a huge cardboard box filled with coffee and doughnuts.

Intense screaming!

Sure enough, here comes the cab again, stopping this time. Out hopped Marc, carrying the goodies, and a pretty woman with dark curly hair, introduced as Susan, Barry's public relations person.

"Barry didn't want you guys to freeze to death out here," Marc said, a young, handsome guy with short, curly brown hair and blue eyes. "So, he sent these over."

More screams. I was in more danger of losing my hearing then of freezing to death.

Marc hung around for a few minutes, answering questions. Barry sent his best wishes and looked forward to meeting us tomorrow. He was back at the hotel, sleeping. He had many exciting projects planned in the coming year: a new album, a TV special and a new tour.

Marc took a picture of the entire group before leaving. Barry wanted to see who his really bizarre fans were, I suppose.

We thanked them for the surprise, sending our thanks to Barry as well. He really did care about his fans.

Before indulging in the coffee and doughnuts, several fans took pictures of the food (and even the cardboard boxes), to be forever affectionately known as "Barry's Buns". A few leftovers were saved as souvenirs (perhaps even eventually bronzed?).

That incident alone made the frosty camp-out worthwhile. When other fans, trickling into line during the night, heard of the visit, they kicked themselves for not being there. But even I had to admit that the best was yet to come.

I didn't sleep at all that night. Vicki returned to the warmth of her car, her cold suddenly reappearing, while Chris snored soundly in his sleeping bag.

I was too excited to sleep. I stayed awake, watching the stars shine and the growing wonder of dawn.

My night was spent thinking of ways to stay warm: my bed back home and of Liv. Wouldn't Liv love this! For sure she would think Americans were crazy. I wished she were there with me. It was her dream to meet Barry too. I was determined that even though she couldn't be there, Barry would know of Liv. I had to thank him for being such an important part of our lives.

I imagined what the parking lot would look like in several hours. One word came to mind: Bedlam! I tried to convince myself that I was actually going to meet Barry. How many people get the chance to meet the one person they always wanted to meet? I was lucky in life, to meet many of my heroes- Bobby Rydell as a kid, Bobby Wine, and down the road, Pat Croce, former owner of the Philadelphia 76ers.

What would I say to Barry? There was so much to say. I wanted to tell him all of our crazy stories with ticket lines, parties and how I had made so many nice friends through his music. I wanted him to know how much I loved certain songs, what his reactions were to different moments in his career. So many questions so little time to ask.

I knew I only had a moment to say whatever I wanted to say before moving on. What was the most important thing I could say to the guy I've wanted to meet for the last fourteen years?

Well, my prediction came true. By morning there were hundreds of fans in line. Thank goodness the weather was kind. Sunny and cold. The crowds were really gathering after Barry's radio interview earlier that morning. Many who didn't know of the book signing knew now.

There were some familiar faces in the crowd, fans I had met from previous concerts. The dreaded "Quarter Noters" finally appeared, trying to bully their way to the head of the line, claiming that honor by being the "official" fan club of the area.

The ploy didn't work. We stood our ground, literally. We didn't spend seventeen hours waiting overnight in line for nothing.

By noon, two gray limos arrived. Barry and company were whisked to the rear of the store. Also arriving was an army of television, radio and newspaper people. All of a sudden I didn't like being first in line. Reporters questioned as to why I was there.

I forgot my reply, saying something like I always loved Barry's music, and couldn't pass up the chance of a lifetime to meet him.

By now, I was running on excitement alone. With no sleep, I felt like a zombie but the sheer thrill of the moment kept me going. This was what I was waiting for.

Susan, Barry's public relations person I met the night before, was standing outside the door with several security guards, waiting for the cue to start leaving five people in at a time.

I wasn't sure if I would have enough time to tell Barry about Liv, so I quickly related the story to Susan, asking her to please tell Barry if she remembered. She thought our relationship was special and agreed to let Barry know.

With 12:30 approaching, shoppers drifted by the huge line, wondering what was going on. "Barry who?" some asked, while others gasped, "Here? You're kidding?"

The line stretched as far as the eye could see. People gazed into the bookstore window, shouting, "I see him He's in there, all right!" as the line screamed and squealed.

The doors finally opened and the first five of us, headed by yours truly and Vicki, followed an older, sharply dressed man from the publishing company through the small store.

What was I thinking? I wasn't nervous, probably too tired and happy to be anxious. My thoughts drifted to Liv.

Emerging from the rows of book selves, there were bright lights ahead. Television cameras and lights were everywhere. They wanted to record whom this mysterious person was, the first to greet Barry on the entire book tour. I blushed.

There were all sorts of people in business suits and dresses, publishing people and Barry's crew. Marc smiled at me. Giving a little wave. And there, standing behind a small walnut table, wearing a beige tweed suit and tie, was Barry Manilow.

My first thought was, "Wait! Shouldn't he be on an album cover or something?" He seemed taller, for some reason.

He looked at me and cheerfully said "Hi!"

"Hi, Barry!" I replied, wheeling to the table, Vicki behind me, nearly fainting. Suddenly, it was like taking another Math exam. My mind went blank. I forgot everything I had planned to say. Instead I muttered, "How's it going?"

We shook hands as Barry sat down. "What's your name?" he asked, and I mumbled a star-struck "Greg". I handed him my book, and as he signed the cover I blurted out "Barry, I have to tell you this real quick," while expecting the security guards to hustle me away, in handcuffs.

"Sure, go ahead," Barry, said, still signing.

"Well, I began breathlessly, "I belong to the fan club and..."

"Oh, really?" he answered, still signing.

"Yes, and they started a pen pal program to match people together who love your music, "I speeded up, trying to condense the entire relationship into ten seconds. "So, I wrote in, got a nice pen pal from Norway, and she visited me during the summer."

"Great!" Barry replied, finally looking up and smiling. He was finished autographing my book.

"Yeah, and she hopes to return next summer, and who knows?" I stammered, coming to a dead-halt to the story.

"Great! He said in amazement, turning to the people around him. "Did you hear that? Isn't that great? I love when I can be involved!"

"She said to tell you hi, "I said. "Our dream is to see you in concert someday, together".

"I'm sure you will," he replied, grinning.

Why couldn't we just have lunch together, talk about music, and let everyone else go home?

"By the way, will you be playing Oslo on this tour?" I asked. It was a dumb question but one which seemed to make sense at the time. I guess all the times Liv wrote, "I wish Barry would come to Norway again" finally got to me.

"Who knows?" Barry shrugged, handing me the signed book.

"Well, we just wanted you to know how much we love your music, and thanks for bringing us together."

"Thanks, " Barry said, still beaming. "Good luck!"

"Thanks," I said, turning to leaving, thinking he had enough of me. On to the next five hundred people in line, starting with the hyperventilating Vicki.

But then Barry called me back. "What's your pen pal's name?"

"Liv-Karin".

"Well, tell Liv I said hi, " he said in closing, waving so long.

"I will. .Bye!" I said, almost running over several toes of reporters as I departed the scene.

It happened so fast, and then it was over. Waiting seventeen hours in the freezing cold was worth it. That's what I told the reporters who waited for my reactions outside the store.

Once outside, I read the inscription on the book cover:

Gregg,

All Best,

Barry Manilow.

It didn't matter if he spelled my name wrong. I had wonderful memories of an unbelievable time, which would last forever.

Vicki met him next, and she was still breathless by the time she met us outside the store. She told Barry that she had been outside all night with a cold, just to meet him.

"You poor thing," he consoled. "Go home and take a Co-Tylenol and go to bed."

"I was this close to his nose!" she whined. "It was fantastic!"

Once home, I called Liv in Norway, relating the entire adventure in a few minutes. She was happy for me and very flattered that Barry asked about her. She also was happy I didn't forget her. How could I? No one was more important then Liv.

Maybe someday we would meet him together. If not, it was still nice to know that he knew of us, and was happy we had found each other.

I didn't bother to get up at six the next morning to hear my explanation why I was waiting in line all night to meet Barry Manilow. At least Vicki said I sounded great on the radio.

Vicki and Chris got married in May of the following year. The wedding was perfect, except for Barry's absence. They had a baby boy down the road, named Barry. Vicki claimed she didn't name him after Barry Manilow. It just worked out that way (yeah, right!).

I sent Liv flowers for her birthday, wishing her well on both her upcoming final exams and her check-up, I was praying to St. Jude for her, the patron saint of hopeless causes. She certainly wasn't "hopeless' but if he could help me [pass math that semester, he could do anything.

On the night of June 16 I called Liv to find out the results of her medical terms. She reported that the cysts had disappeared! Even the doctors were amazed.

Somebody up there had to be on our side.

Liv's student loan finally came through. But she needed to work part of the summer for expenses. We decided to meet again in late August, this time for only two weeks before school began. Two weeks with Liv was better then none. We both looked forward to a well-deserved vacation at the end of summer.

Meanwhile, I worked extra hours at the nursing home, getting ready for my last semester of school. I was preparing for graduation. Most of my hard courses, like Math, were behind me. I couldn't wait to graduate now, with so much to look forward to now in the future. Unless something disastrous happened, I would graduate from college in December of the upcoming semester.

Liv got a job at a publishing company in Oslo. I missed her more then ever, remembering just a year ago and our special summer together. This summer was too lonely and too long.

August 31- the day I was looking forward to. Welcome back, Liv!

Coming out of customs, there she was, looking as stunning as ever, in a beige outfit. This time we didn't shake hands as before. Instead we hugged, the warm embrace we had dreamed of all winter.

It took Liv a little longer to get over her jet lag this time. My annual bout with hay fever was acting up. So we sneezed and yawned a lot for the first few days (fun couple, eh?).

Our favorite restaurant, going to the movies, cuddling late at night- the memories were alive again. After taking the winter to think, our love remained strong. We missed the holidays and special times together but we also missed sharing those everyday experiences, which can make or break a relationship.. We couldn't continue to live for summer alone. How could we know if it was forever when we were always far apart?

Sooner or later we had to stay together longer then two months or two weeks. Graduation was approaching and more decisions needed to be made. Our relationship was certainly different. "Normal" couples worry about money, what to have for dinner. We did too, but things like visas started creeping into our lives.

Liv liked America. Her English was better then mine. She didn't anticipate many problems finding a job after graduation. She would miss her family but she missed me more when we were apart.

So, we took an important step towards our goal that summer- we got engaged.

Were we going too fast? After her previous engagement I could understand her hesitation. I could accept if she suggested, "let's think about this a little more". Married to me, life wouldn't be easy. She would share the stares, the pain and the hurt. She would encounter obstacles which I met everyday. I didn't have the right to ask her to endure all that. However, knowing my situation, it didn't stop her from saying, "Yes, I will marry you. I love you too".

From pen pals to an engagement? I was happy; sure she was the right one, not wanting to lose her, yet still having feeling of doubt, mostly in myself.

Everyone was surprised, especially when they saw the diamond. It wasn't expensive, I couldn't afford it, but it was the love that counted.

Was it just a 'friendship ring"? They can't be serious. Why would Liv want me? Couldn't she find someone "normal"? What was wrong with her? Was she marrying me just to get her American citizenship, only to dump me in the end?

That was the kind of whispers we heard. We didn't care; we only cared about each other.

Maybe Liv could have found anyone she wanted. Maybe my disability didn't matter to her, nor did time and distance. And maybe, just maybe, she really did love me.

Another tearful goodbye awaited us. This time I was sure Liv would return- next year. Until then, our letters would link our love, as always. Missing her would never get any easier.

Little did I know that we would meet again sooner then planned, in a very special way.

During the autumn I started sending out resumes. I was hoping to get lucky, as most people told me I would have to travel or live in Philadelphia to find a good job in the social work field. I soon began to realize that Laurie wasn't going to be around forever for transportation. I had to take the next big step in my independence.

Not being able to drive still bugged me. I wanted to drive, yearning for even more independence, remembering Wheelchair Willie and other disabled people in my past that drove successfully. I needed this, both for my personal life, but for my career as well.

Willie had shown me how to drive a few times in his van, when we were car-pooling together "It's easy, " he would quip. "You can even drive with your belly," he laughed- and he did. He wanted to give me the confidence I lacked. I have a good pair of hands. I didn't necessarily need my legs to drive.

So, with my confidence at an all-time high, I contacted Vocational Rehabilitation and asked them to hook me up with adaptive driving. They were only too happy to help me, now that I was almost through my four years of college. So they got me an evaluation with Bryn Mawr Rehabilitation Hospital, one of the best in the area. I was looking forward to it.

On an overcast, rainy morning, Mom and I arrived at the sprawling, one story hospital. It seemed like a cool place, ideal for someone confined to a chair. Plenty of parking spaces (not an able-bodied person stealing a handicapped space, like in the real world), automatic doors and ramps. This was a place where disability was the norm, not the minority. With so much accessibility I wished the outside world could take a lesson from the facility.

The purpose of this evaluation was to determine if I really could drive. If so, then what kind of modifications would be needed? What kind of adaptable car would I need? Or would a van be more realistic (yet more expensive), with a wheel chair lift and hand-controls, the kind Willie had?

Mom took me down for the evaluation. I took a physical, then an eye exam and a coordination exam. I thought they were just going to give me a driving booklet, maybe a written test, send me home to study, then return to see if I could actually drive.

Instead, they put me in an accessible car- equipped with hand-controls- and with an instructor by my side, told me to take a spin around the parking lot. They pulled the compact gray vehicle under the roof at the main entrance as I transferred into the car. Mom watched, helpless, probably more nervous then I was.

The ol' sink or swim theory. While we were already in the car, the instructor showed me the basic controls, and then suggested we take a spin around the lot. It was a pleasant idea-until I realized that I would be doing the driving.

I was scared to death. I never was behind the wheel before. I wasn't sure which was the brake and which control was the gas. In my anxiety, my mind turned to mush (just like Math class and meeting Barry Manilow). I choked. Plus, because of my short stature, I had a hard time looking over the hood, let alone see the rear-view mirror, even with the help of cushions. This was my first time in a driver's seat, and it felt so strange. It was like a dream, a taste of what I was missing most of my life.

I think most of their cases were newly disabled people, like Willie, who already knew the general idea of driving, and who had driven before their particular illness or accident. I was new to the entire thing, very raw.

I fumbled with the ignition to start the car before going anywhere. We were in trouble. The brakes screeched as we pulled away from the building. The car jerked as I tried to remember the different hand controls while trying to steer at the same time. The controls were very sensitive. Since I was left-handed, everything was backwards. I began to believe I was one of those guys who couldn't chew gum and walk at the same time- if I could walk.

At least I could always say that I actually drove a car, not well, but I drove. The parking lot was full, which seemed odd to me. Don't you practice in an empty lot? I imagined learning to drive in an empty lot, like a supermarket lot, as my brothers had, late at night. I remember sitting in the backseat, thinking it was funny when my brother nearly drove up on a curb.

I wasn't laughing now.

I thought I was doing fairly well at first. Oh, I drove on the grass occasionally, and I kept forgetting to stay on my side of the road, little things like that.

Then it happened. The car didn't go the way I wanted it to, as if it had a mind of its own (at least one of us did). The instructor, who had his own set of over-riding controls, grabbed the wheel, swerving the car out of the way- just in time before hitting a parked car.

I was embarrassed, but even more frightened. The instructor was even a little shaken. I didn't hit the car, but thoughts of "what if" haunted me. Right then, I never wanted to drive again, even though I did drive back to the main entrance - still in one piece.

The thunderstorm pelting sheets of rain didn't help matters. I was trying to peer thought the windshield between raindrops, trying to remember the hand-controls, trying to listen to the instructor beside me, trying not to hit a car in the lot, my mind swirling, in another world. I was totally overwhelmed.

I breathed a big sigh of relief when we returned to the main entrance. I would have nightmares about that day for years to come, just as I had nightmares about my childhood fractures and surgeries. Luckily, I didn't hit any cars or people.

The verdict was that maybe I could eventually drive, but needed a lot of work. No kidding!

I needed lessons-thirty of them, to be exact. And I needed to read my manual. I felt like a failure.

I never went back for another test or lesson. I knew that was a mistake, Not being able to drive would haunt me in the future, not only with jobs, but in my personal life too. After overcoming so many challenges in my life, I felt so low, having failed. And the worst part was knowing, deep down inside, that I could do it!

I didn't look back at my driving experience as a complete failure, just another challenge to overcome someday, a goal. I had to accept that maybe I couldn't do everything in life, not necessarily giving up, but there were some things I had to deal with and accept.

Sure, I knew it was a cop-out. I felt embarrassed when I saw people far more disabled then I was who were able to drive. People who used only their tongue, or a few fingers to steer. Amazing! I admired their determination, their sheer will to achieve independence.

But I couldn't allow this one episode get me down. I had come too far. If it was meant to be, then so be it. I learned some humility too;

that it's all right to ask others for help if needed, and still not feel dependent. I learned to take advantage of the bus, eventually of Paratransit, after the Americans With Disabilities Act was passed, which allowed disabled folks to ride the special vans, along with the elderly.

Again, all I had to do was ask. I learned a long time ago there were good people out there, willing to help.

I graduated from West Chester University with a grade point average of 3.56- not bad. I left with mixed emotions, happy I had made it, after four long years of study; sad to be leaving my friends, leaving the carefree days of school behind and on to the real world of working.

Taking my very last exam was probably the easiest part of those final weeks of school. The red tape of graduating- verifying my credits, the multitude of paperwork, ordering my cap and gown- was work in itself. It was tough not only getting into college but getting out as well.

One thing I especially took pride in was my college ring. Ok, maybe it was corny, but to me, it was a symbol of achievement. I couldn't afford gold, so I ordered a silver ring, with my birthstone, topaz, in the middle. Inscribed were my name, my degree and the year I graduated. Even later in life, as my college memories faded, I would wear that ring. It reminded me how far I had come. It reminded me, especially during the future times when I just wanted to give up, not to give up. It reminded me of all the hard work and discrimination I overcame, not only in college but also during my entire life.

All I needed was to look at my right hand, if I ever need a spark of motivation. It was a constant reminder of achievement, and I was always proud to wear it.

I couldn't believe I was finished! I gave it my best shot. I was proud of what I had accomplished. It sure wasn't easy, but it sure was worth it.

I felt like shouting. Instead, a quiet calm settled over me. I remembered everything I went through since Willie encouraged me to enter college four years ago.

I recalled all the classes, the term papers, the exams, the long nights studying, the frosty early mornings, the icy, steep hills, which we climbed each day, and most of all, the friends I had made.

I recalled the many times I wanted to give up, and didn't. Something kept me going. I remembered Dad, how proud he would have been. Mom, her eternal love and support. Laurie, for her great compassion and friendship, and everyone else who helped me on the way.

I also thought of Liv, for her love, for being so special, for giving me yet another incentive to work hard, something to look forward to in my life.

At first it was difficult being an older, returning student. Tough making new friends, blending in with the younger students, adjusting to school after so many years. It surprised me, just how far I had come in so short a time. I hoped to show those who said I would never amount to anything that I could do it. More importantly, I proved to myself that I could do just about anything if only I tried.

Now I hoped people would look at my intelligence first, not just my legs. I hoped that my success would inspire others in my situation- the disabled, the hopeless, the poor- all of which I was. Now I was a "Willie", a role model, and an example to others. Knowing I had such a responsibility to live up to kept me fighting.

I intended to put my new degree to good use by helping others. That was my goal, my dream, and I wasn't going to change now.

Dear Laurie! Her future plans included working while perhaps returning to school someday for her Masters. She also needed the experience and the money. "It will be good to finally get out of poverty," she said.

All she ever wanted was a decent life to care for herself and her kids. Now, thanks to a lot of hard work and determination, she was finally going to get that chance.

We promised to keep in touch but I knew Laurie and I were to part ways. She was huge for me, not only for transportation, but also for her friendship. She guided me in times of trouble, when I was having problems with Fox, when I started my relationship with Liv, always supportive. I would never forget her. She eventually moved away to New England and found a job in a nursing home there. We would exchange Christmas cards and occasional letters but she moved on with her life. She had earned her degree, leaving welfare and poverty behind. Although she wasn't going to make much money, she was happy. Most of all, she achieved success and respect, a major victory in itself.

I was so proud on Graduation Day. I thought of all the people in my past. I remembered the lady at Penn who predicted that I would never make anything of my life. I hoped my Dad would have been proud. Thinking back just four years earlier I was nowhere in life. Now, I had my degree, a girlfriend, more independence, and I had a long way to go.

Laurie and I both wanted to continue in school for our Masters. But we both needed to start paying off student loans. Plus we wanted to get out in the field and start using our talents to help others. We were tired of studying, exams, and the stress of school. It would be nice to have weekends and evenings free again.

Finally, I was a social worker! My dream come true! I was determined to be a kind and caring professional, no matter what. I had been on both sides of the fence- client, patient, and now caseworker. That experience, along with my life experience of disability, would help me through my career and through life, as I braved the world of employment.

After recharging my batteries over the holidays, I began searching for a job. It was nice to wind down after the semester, but as usual, after a few days of doing nothing, I grew restless.

It took a while adjusting to life without school. No more homework, studying late at night, no final exams. Now I could put my books on the shelf for future use, once I gathered the scattered lot of them. Actually I never sold a book, as often students did at the end of semesters. I took care of mine well, because they treated me well, and I could always refer back to them as needed.

I got my final transcript in the mail. And when my long awaited diploma finally arrived I displayed it proudly in my room. That beautiful piece of paper with the fancy writing- it symbolized so much of what I had worked for.

The positions of social worker at both the local nursing home and hospital were filled. They were both jobs I wanted, jobs I had done before, and done well. I loved working with the residents, patients and staff at each facility. Now it was all a matter of patience, timing and luck.

I continued to work at the nursing home on Saturdays. I wanted to keep my foot in the door, just in case an opening occurred after graduation. Plus, It would be hard totally leaving the residents. They planted the seed that I could go from a volunteer to become a professional. They showed me how much a simple, kind word could do to encourage someone in need. They gave me something to live and to work for. Whatever good I did over the years- the room visits to say hello and cheer, the reading groups, the counseling and encouragement, just taking time to listen, when others didn't have the time- was given back to me many times by the residents. I always felt so fortunate to go out in the sunshine with freedom and independence. They taught me that my life wasn't so bad after all.

We would miss each other. We shared much hope, laughter, tears and love over the years. I saw much illness and pain, yet I also shared in so much happiness too.

Although the faces changed, each resident touched my life in some way. They taught me far more then a textbook ever could. They treated me as an equal, without the discrimination I often encountered on the outside. In fact, many of the nursing home resident's thought, because of my wheel chair, that I was a resident as well, asking, "What room are you in?"

They showed me that it was all right to be a disabled person, to accept it, make the best of it, and go on.

Searching for a job is a job in itself. It is hard work, often degrading, depressing and exhausting.

Many jobs in the social work field required a Masters Degree. Many required being on the road, doing casework outside the office. Without being able to drive I was up the creek without a...car.

I knew it. I needed to learn how to drive someday soon. I was frightened of the new responsibility, which went with independence. But driving was becoming a necessity. Reality dictated that I needed a job to afford a car, bit I also needed a car in order to hold down a job.

First came the job. Car-pooling or public transportation were possibilities until I got my license. But eventually, I knew that driving was a must.

Even I was surprised at the discrimination I was facing in my job hunting. I wrote to Liv late in the evenings, expressing my frustrations in dealing with stereotypes on a daily basis. I wasn't going to accept this discrimination, those employers who judged me by my disability rather then my ability. My success in education was helping to break down some of those barriers of prejudice.

That professor I had met in my community college was right. He advised me that, despite all of his academic achievements, he was still judged by the color of his skin. I would also be judged by my disability, like it or not. I would have to deal with it, face it, and work hard to prove myself.

Still, many misconceptions remained. Stereotypes such as the physically challenged being thought of as mentally challenged as well; I had experienced these stereotypes before, that disabled people shouldn't be married, shouldn't have sex, or that we are less cheerful and happy and hard-working then so called able bodied people in society.

As society learned more about the disabled, with help from the Americans With Disabilities Act becoming more prominent in society, others found that we do have the same feelings and emotions as anyone else. With more education and as the disabled became less foreign, the more comfortable society tends to become with the physically challenged, and vice versa. I hoped that my efforts towards independence would help to erase the misconceptions and strengthen the positive image of the disabled.

All I wanted was a chance to prove myself. But it became so discouraging that I started looking for work outside of my field. I didn't want to do that. I was trained in social work. That is why I went to school, and it was what I was good at.

Still, there weren't many social work openings in my area. So I had to go where the money was. I applied for jobs as a dispatcher for the police department, a secretary (even though my typing sucked) and a telephone operator. But either I didn't have the proper training or I was over-qualified. I wasn't looking to make a fortune, but the money being offered wasn't even worth getting off Social Security for, thus losing my health benefits.

Here I was, fresh out of college, with excellent grades and referrals, yet no one would give me a chance. I had to keep trying, have patience and not give up hope. I needed a job soon, especially with Liv coming over. Being broke and unemployed wasn't exactly a great way to begin a marriage.

I was most surprised at the lack of accessibility for a wheel chair bound person during my job search. I constantly went to combat with steps to get to interviews. Other places I had to use the backdoor or service elevator.

I let my resume stand on its own merit, not mentioning my disability on the phone when I responded to ads. But upon arriving at the interview, I often found surprising-or not so surprising- stares and an inaccessible environment. I had to try even harder to sell myself. I was ready to work but were they ready for me?

The situation was pretty degrading. There were more and more disabled people out there in the work force, trailblazers all, yet not enough changes. Stereotypical attitudes were far harder to change then mere physical barriers.

My friends kept their eyes open for jobs. I went to what seemed like hundreds of interviews and job fairs, sending out tons of resumes. I used to turn to the sports section as soon as the paper arrived. Now it was the classifieds.

Then a problem concerning an over-payment of benefits occurred with Social Security. The claim was that I had made too much money from my part-time job at the nursing home during my college years, and the verdict was that I had to repay all of that money, all of those disability checks.

I was disabled. I would always be disabled. I made very minimal income during those years, just enough to buy schoolbooks, most of which went into my education needs. I had returned to school to get off Social Security someday, instead of staying home and collecting checks. Now I understood why other disabled people were so frustrated and didn't work. What was the use?

I was on the other side of the fence again, the client instead of the worker.

I l felt like a common criminal, required to reveal my personal history, asked to show up at the office to "prove I was really disabled". This insensitivity made me more aware of the need to be more sensitive to clients. It eventually made me a better social worker.

I couldn't wait to find work and support myself. But it seemed as though I was being penalized for striving for independence, as though I was being told to "stay disabled".

I was determined to fight for my rights. I wasn't going to let them take away what I had rightfully been entitled to, especially my dignity.

The problem still remained that I didn't see myself as disabled, as being so different then others, but society reminded me-I was different. Every time I got my courage up, I was blown away again by disappointment. I just couldn't give up.

With so much frustration in my life, I tried to call Liv. I often called her to say hello, but this time was different. Hearing her voice always cheered me and gave me hope.

I tried to call all weekend with no luck. She was due for another physical check-up, and I wanted to find out the results.

I finally got through-to Liv's Mom. I had spoken to her before, and this conversation was no different. She didn't speak English, and my Norwegian was lousy, so it made for a pretty fun talk.

"Hello", "Liv", and "Goodbye" were about the only words that didn't need translation. I did remember the phrase "ikke me". After hanging up, I quickly searched my Norwegian dictionary, finding the phrase "ikke me", which meant "not here" (or close to it).

Later that night Liv called back. "Not here" meant Liv had been visiting her aunt in Oslo for the weekend.

Liv's check-up went fine, however she was growing restless. After graduation she had moved most of her belongings back home. She couldn't believe how many things she had accumulated over the years: books, plates, stuffed animals (my fault). Moving was a big job. Then she had to move again when she got an apartment in Oslo after she found a job.

Moving was the only part of which she wasn't looking forward to when she was ready to come to the States permanently. Packing and shipping her things would be expensive as well as a lot of work.

Liv didn't know exactly when she would be moving over. She planned to visit again the upcoming summer, and then we would see what happened. She still had some things to straighten out at home- her finances, her visa, and her information from the embassy.

Although I missed Liv terribly and wanted to see her soon, I also wanted her to take her time before making the big move. Only when she was truly ready.

What did her family think? Sure, they would miss her. I imagined how my family would feel if I was living abroad, especially with someone they never met before. I imagined how I would feel too, having to cope with the culture shock and missing home.

We had some advantages though: Liv liked America, she had been here before, her English was excellent, she knew what to expect, and most of all, and she wanted to move over. I know it would take time to adjust. We planned on visiting Norway when we could- together. And her family and friends looked forward to visiting us in the States.

Whenever I started to worry, Liv would tell me not to. She loved me, and everything would be all right.

I went six months before finally finding a job. For a while it was frustrating, looking for work, still on disability. I went to school to get off disability, yet here I was, still in the same situation, and now without school to fall back on.

Then it happened. I scanned the classifieds one evening and found an opening form a caseworker at another local nursing home.

I applied to a really nice nursing home nearby, called the Montgomery County Geriatric & Rehabilitation Center. It was the best place around and only ten minutes from home. My dream job, working back at the Manor, where I had started as a volunteer, worked part-time, and eventually did one of my internships, was filled. I had to wait my chance, but until then I hoped to get the opening at the Geriatric Center.

Everything seemed perfect. The ad asked for someone with a degree in Social Work (which I had), with nursing home experience (which I had), and with extensive experience working with older adults (which I also had). The salary and benefits were great. It was the answer to my prayers.

I was excited when I saw the ad. This was MY job! It was the job I was trained for, the job I had worked so hard for, the job I wanted.

I rushed my resume in the mail, and I immediately called for an interview. I felt confident. I was sure I could handle anything that the job had to offer.

It was a really big facility, over 500 beds, a sprawling place in nearby Royersford, only a few miles from home. When I interviewed for the job I was really nervous, my first interview ever, and I really wasn't myself. I knew that I didn't have the experience, as was my downfall in so many other interviews. My college record was impressive, but I just didn't have the experience. But how does one get the experience if no one will give you a chance?

Surprisingly, after what I thought was a terrible interview, I got another call back from the Geriatric Center. I learned the position of caseworker was down to one other person and me. I prayed I would get it and waited for good news.

What a relief it would be to have a job! It would be so nice to forget about resumes and interviews, the anxiety and pressure off my mind. Wouldn't Liv be proud? We could finally plan for the future together.

Well, they did call me back-but not with the news I wanted. Diane, the Social Service Director, was a very nice person, and gently explained to me, that although she admired my grit and determination, and was impressed by my life experience and college grades, she was really looking for someone with more experience in the field. The job went to the other applicant.

Discouraged, I moved on. It would have been an ideal position for me. Now it was back to sending out more resumes and trying to get lucky. . I was still being offered jobs such as stuffing envelopes. Back to more ads and stereotypes. I prayed hard for courage and strength.

I tried to keep my chin up and didn't want Liv to know I was failing. She was also looking for work, in the same situation, needing a job just to pay back her student loan. For a while, she was back working in the bookstore again. Then she landed a job with a big law firm in Oslo, and I was so happy for her. She still planned on visiting next summer, and the ultimate goal of moving to America, but for now, she needed to work, which I understood.

I was getting more and more depressed, and began to believe those who said I would have to go into the city to find a job. Then inspiration hit.

I remembered a teacher at my old community college. He taught a night class, once a week. He was the head of Aging in nearby Norristown, and I recalled he told me at the time if I ever needed a favor in the future to call him. Ed and I became good friends, and I took him up on the offer.

I called him out of the blue one day and was surprised he remembered me. I told him that I had graduated and now I was looking for work. He couldn't promise anything but he asked me to visit him at the office the following Monday.

I did so, and that very day I had a job. Now, things weren't as I had hoped. I still didn't know how I was going to get back and forth each day. I still couldn't drive, and didn't expect Mom to drive me each day. The bus route stopped five blocks away from the office, located in the center of Norristown, a town somewhat larger then Phoenixville. But Ed wanted me to work for him so badly, he agreed, until I worked out a transportation solution, that I could take a taxi to and from work, and that the county would pick up the tab. Since he was a big wheel in the county, he thought there wouldn't be a problem. So, until I could think of another way, or arrange another car pool situation like Laurie, that is what I did.

The other concern was the job itself. It really wasn't a social work job, what I went to school for. It was more into computers. (Computers again). I really wasn't sure what my responsibilities were, even to this day. Something about checking numbers and coordinating schedules for county agencies such as Meals on Wheels. I think good-hearted Ed just wanted me to have a good job, and basically gave me anything for the time being. I didn't want to stay on disability, so I took whatever he offered me.

The pay was good, the benefits even better, and there was room to grow. Most of all, it was a permanent, full-time job.

Ironically enough, the local hospital called me about a week later, offering me a temporary position at the hospital, filling in for the summer. I really wanted to work at the hospital. I liked my experience there during my college internship. It was close to home. I wouldn't have to worry about transportation.

But the hospital couldn't promise me a full-time position after the summer. In September I would be back to where I was before, searching the want ads. It was a tough decision- take the steady job, which I wasn't totally sure of, or go with my heart, and take the temporary job, and hope to get lucky.

Taking a temporary position would also mess up my Social Security benefits, which I was still trying to straighten out, although I didn't know back then, there was a "trial work period" where I could work, and yet receive benefits for a time, until I found a full-time position.

I stayed with the job in Norristown, although that little voice inside, which I should have known to listen to, told me it was wrong. The hospital was disappointed that I turned them down, but they understood. I just hoped I did the right thing.

My very first supervisor was a real nasty witch. Her daughter worked in the office with her She was always on my back about not counting numbers correctly or just being bored. But it was true: I didn't understand my job or what I was there for, and neither did anyone else. Ed had me on the payroll until something better opened up. As it turned out, this "organization" job was the same job this supervisor was hoping to get. Now here I was, green out of school, really not knowing what I was doing, and I had taken her coveted position.

If I only knew, she could have had her position. I didn't want to be into computers, or planning or politics or anything else. I just wanted to do social work, my passion in life and the reason why I went to college and worked so hard for so long.

This lady was nasty to everyone. She was overweight, and seemed to have a real self-esteem problem, so she took out her attitude on everyone else. She happened to be a good organizer, plus she buffaloed Ed into thinking she was a great person. No one else in the office had the guts to tell him how she really was, and I learned a lot about office politics. I kept my mouth shut and didn't even tell Ed how bullying she was to me; I was so intimidated by her. Plus now that I was off disability, what if I lost my job? Could I get back on benefits? Did I make a big mistake, taking this position?

I remember one day, a group of us went out for lunch because it was the supervisor's' daughters' birthday. I almost had to go, like it or not, even though I was withdrawing into my shell again, quiet and intimidated. What hurt the most was when the supervisor had to fold my wheelchair and put it in the trunk, then came back growling, "If I hurt my back I'll get worker's comp, " she whined. "They don't pay me enough to do this crap."

I felt so low. I didn't ask to go to this party, nor did I want to.

That year, they had their annual Christmas party at a place which was not accessible for a wheelchair. It was actually suggested that instead of carrying the wheelchair up the stairs to the banquet room, or maybe finding another hall that was accessible, that I ride the waiter's dummy elevator upstairs. I felt humiliated. They made a big scene, because I was their only handicapped employee at the time, and it looked like I was the troublemaker. I ended up not going to the party at all.

I started to regret not taking the summer job at the Phoenixville Hospital. I wasn't happy, full-time job or not. What was really important?

After several months of this harassment, I had it. I finally went to Ed, and explained that I wasn't happy. I appreciated his kindness, the fact he got me a job, and I knew the taxi ride each day was costing the county a bundle. But I started looking elsewhere. Even if it meant going back on disability, I wasn't sure how much more unhappiness I could take.

Once Ed finally knew just how unhappy I was, he arranged for an opening in the office's Intake and Referral department. I was never so happy!

First, it meant I had a new supervisor, a young girl named Debbie. Second, it was more of a social work kind of job, answering phones, giving out information, referring people to organizations, counseling people who needed help from the streets. I accepted the job and quickly loved it.

The small group of caseworkers with me was friendly and fun to work with. Each call, each case was different and a challenge. I learned so much, as I had at the hospital, with different cases, different ages, and different clients. Just never knew who or what would enter the office. It kept the job exciting yet at times dangerous too.

I'll never forget the time two guys had a knife fight in our lobby. The Aging offices were located on the 8th floor. Security was down in the lobby. It would have been nothing for a guy to sneak a gun upstairs and shoot someone if he really wanted to. The knife fight was about two guys who came in from the streets, looking for monthly hotel vouchers. When one didn't play the game and act out the routine they planned, they were rolling in the floor in the lobby. I just tried to stay out of the way.

Another time I met with a young black guy one day, nothing unusual. He was looking for County assistance, either money or voucher or both. I took him into the interview room, alone, which was nothing unusual. About fifteen minutes later two gentlemen wearing dark suits appeared outside the office and asked to speak with the caseworker who had helped that young guy just moments before. That caseworker was me.

I learned the two gentlemen in dark suits were FBI agents, and the guy they were trailing was wanted for murder. They asked me what he wanted, and I told them the truth. I saw in the local papers about a week later that he was finally arrested and was eventually convicted of a murder.

We had many seriously mentally ill people drift into the office, many homeless, looking for shelter, food or whatever provisions we could offer. Our office was located in a really nice part of town, right across from the County courthouse. Well-dressed lawyers and other professional people were all around that block. But go a little ways down the block, where a few other co-workers and me would sometimes go for lunch, and there were hookers and druggies and homeless galore. A totally different world- only a block away.

Well, usually around the first of the month, when everyone knew the County had new money and vouchers to give away, the line would form outside our office on the first of the month. We would literally give away the free stuff we had to offer, and then the rest of the month was pretty quiet. But one time a smelly man in dirty, ragged clothes came in late in the day for money. By then, there was none left. I had to tell him the bad news. He didn't like that news, and threatened me. I called my supervisor and they asked him to leave the office immediately.

When I wheeled down the hall to the elevator to go home, meeting my taxi in the parking garage, this guy was waiting for me. He boarded the elevator with me, without saying a word, but I was scared. Luckily there were other people on board with us, but they got off before we reached the parking garage.

Alone, he again asked me for money, but I told him he would have to come back the next day to the office and I would see what I could do for him. As he started to approach me in the elevator-who knows what he was going to do- the elevator door opened. We had reached the parking garage, and luckily, waiting outside was a security guard. I got out, met my cab, as the man rode back upstairs to the lobby, escorted by the guard. He never did come back the next day, and I never saw him again.

There were some good aspects to the job. Like the time I helped an unwed mother, only a teenager, find diapers for her little baby. The baby was only a few months old, and the mother, either homeless or living on practically nothing, couldn't afford diapers. Rather then give her money, which we learned would often go instead for drugs or alcohol, I called different stores in the area. Finally a toy store locally agreed to donate a box of diapers. The box was slightly damaged during packaging but the diapers were still good. She only had to pick them up, which she agreed to do. It was only as temporary fix, and I hoped she would come back so we could plan a long-term solution to her problem, such as getting her more help, an education or some kind of purpose in life. I sympathized with her, because I was in a seemingly helpless situation only years earlier.

I found that many people wanted to get out of bad situations- abusive relationships, homeless, living at the Salvation Army, with no job, no money, and no clothes. Some had been laid-off from their jobs, or an illness caused their lives to destruct. Others just didn't care, and actually wanted to live on the streets and not work, preferring instead to seek handouts. Others were ill, especially mentally ill, and it saddened me to see these people without help. Some agreed to help when I hooked them up to area agencies, others declined.

It taught me a lesson just how lucky I was, especially to have achieved so much. I helped people with AIDS, people with all sorts of diseases and afflictions, but it didn't bother me. I wasn't really afraid, although we adopted a policy of keeping the interview room door open; just in case someone needed help.

Again, it was good experience and everyday when I went home I felt good inside, knowing I had helped someone in need. It made me feel good that on a bitterly cold night, I had helped someone find a warm bed in a shelter rather then spend the night out in the cold. It was what social work was all about, and I learned a lot of things I could never learn in a classroom.

I really liked my job now. This is what social work was all about, helping others in need. Unfortunately, it wouldn't last very much longer. But in the end, all things happen for a reason.

7. LOOKS LIKE WE MADE IT

I got a call at work one January afternoon from a reporter for one of the television stations in Philadelphia. His name was Mike and he hosted a special segment on the local late news called "Three Wishes", which granted the requests of some very lucky viewers.

The summer before I had written Mike a letter, expressing my wish for Liv and I to meet Barry Manilow someday, this time together. I explained what Barry's music meant to us, how we met, and how we fell in love. I thought it would be terrific if we had a chance to thank Barry together.

Liv knew nothing about my letter. I wanted it to be a surprise. I never thought they would pick my wish, imagining they had to receive hundreds of wishes each week (and they did).

I remembered seeing some really nice stories on the "Three Wishes" segment: a mentally challenged young man getting to meet and skate with his idols, the Philadelphia Flyers hockey club; an area man's lifelong goal of being a disc jockey for a day; a family being reunited for the holidays.

Dreams came true. I never thought mine would. I didn't think my dream was important enough. I still wrote to Mike, because if I didn't believe in my dreams, who would?

My relationship with Liv was so special. She was special. I wanted everyone to know it.

I forgot all about that letter until nearly six months later when I received a call from Mike. All of a sudden I remembered the letter pretty quickly.

Mike loved the letter and really thought my relationship with Liv was something that people would be interested in hearing about. He wanted to do the story the summer before but Barry wasn't on tour. Now he was on tour, with an appearance in Atlantic City only ten days away. He wanted to do the story now, if possible.

I was floored. I couldn't believe the next couple of weeks.

If Liv could make it over by next week, and if Mike could arrange things with Barry and the casino where Barry would be performing, they would do an entire feature on our wish come true: meeting Barry.

Meeting Barry? With Liv? It seemed too good to be true, and

almost was.

The first thing to do was ask Liv if she was willing to visit. Mike would work on the mountains of red tape involved. There was a possibility an airline would fly Liv over for free, in exchange for the publicity.

I couldn't promise Mike that Liv would make it for sure. There was a lot to consider. He didn't promise me that all the arrangements could be ironed out either. But it was a start.

I called Liv, relating the entire crazy story. The plan seemed like a fantasy, a fairy tale, just like our relationship. But we couldn't get carried away with excitement just yet. Problems were on the horizon.

Liv was stunned by the news. This was a chance of a lifetime. She didn't foresee any trouble in taking off from work for a few days. Plus, most of her time in the States would be spent during a weekend. She was willing to endure the long trip and jet lag, for a chance to see me again and to meet Barry.

However, with living expenses still a major problem, she wasn't sure if she would be able to afford the costly airfare, even out of season. Could she get a ticket in time, with only a week to go?

I told her not to worry. I would pay for her trip. I would understand if she couldn't make it. Everything was so rushed and such a surprise. If things couldn't be worked out in time Mike still wanted to do the story in the future, when Liv was in the States and Barry was available.

Liv was excited about the idea. She would check on the airline tickets and call me the next day.

The thought of seeing her again in a week was a wish come true in itself- if everything worked out.

Meanwhile, Mike kept in touch everyday. Everything looked good so far. Liv would fly in for a few days before the show) February 6). The television station would pick us up and whisk us to Atlantic City for dinner, the show, and the meeting with Barry.

It seemed so perfect. Mike would get his story. The Delaware Valley would get to share in a real-life love story. Liv and I would have our wish come true.

Then the wheels started to come off. First, the good news: Liv got her plane ticket but she could only arrive at 1:30pm on February 6- the day of the show.

So, the new plan was to ride to JFK airport in New York, then travel to Atlantic City. I felt terrible that Liv would have to travel so far in just one day, but she didn't complain.

Liv would only be able to stay until the following Monday: three days, on her specially priced ticket. A weekend of fun was better then nothing, and what a weekend it would be!

Still, plans had to be finalized. Some fell through. Mike worked hard to ask an airline to help Liv with her ticket but they refused, saying since she bought her ticket already, and was coming over anyway, they couldn't do anything. I guess the airlines weren't sentimental.

Mike felt bad. He knew about our financial situation. But I assured him it would be worthwhile. I used some of my savings since I started working full-time, some of the money I was saving for a possible accessible van someday. It was the chance of a lifetime.

Then the casino gave Mike a hard time. Even with the free publicity the hotel still hesitated. They didn't believe I was really disabled. They thought the whole thing might be a scam.

Mike pointed out that my disability had little to do with our wish. It was the love story and the connection with Barry, which was the main interest of the story.

Mike rarely did wishes where people asked to meet celebrities. Too many such requests. In fact, there had been several wishes to meet Barry before mine.

This one, Mike noted, was different. My wish was also for Liv. It was a wish of love, and that is why he wanted to make it come true.

Mike was appalled with the crassness of the idea that it may be a put-on. He never met me personally, but there was no question in his mind that I was honest.

The casino pointed out that the show was sold out. Luckily, I had tickets (one of my own, and one of Vicki's- who couldn't go to the show, and sold her ticket to me). Mike conveniently mentioned this to the casino representative. It didn't matter that the seats were way in the back of the theatre. We were there, that's all that mattered.

Why the casino resisted so strongly never became clear, remaining a mystery to Mike as well. Why would they resist such a positive, happy story?

Our plans looked suddenly bleak, especially when the casino said, ticket or no ticket, they wouldn't agree to be the setting for the meeting. Just as suddenly they changed their minds. In one day, everything looked brighter. Mike's tone was optimistic as we ended our conversation that

Friday. He would touch base again on Monday. Only one week until the big day.

As a social worker, I should've been used to red tape. I spent the weekend on needles and pins, yet looking forward to the upcoming week.

Then another snag, this time from a source I never expected in my wildest dreams to resist- Barry.

Mike called on Monday, and immediately I knew from his voice he was the bearer of bad news. Barry seemingly didn't want to meet us. At least that was what his people were implying to Mike.

Mike had heard that Manilow was tough to deal with. Mike was in the business. In his book, Barry even admitted there was a time he used to be cold with the press and public.

But now, he supposedly was a more open, friendly guy with the media and his fans. We had a taste of his kindness the night we camped out at the bookstore ("Barry's Buns"). He had done so much for different charities over the years. He also grew closer to his fans; those who helped turn his career into superstardom, after years of distancing himself from the fans.

I couldn't understand why Barry seemed reluctant to contribute to the story. Mike thought that if Barry did one of these special meetings with fans, he would have to do them all. Still, he often did so many nice things for his fans.

His people asked if I could transfer from my wheelchair to a regular seat. I could, but what difference did that make? Didn't Barry want to be seen with a disabled person?

That was hard to believe, since he had done so much work in previous years for the United Way.

What was it then?

Mike thought the real reason was that Barry's people did not want television cameras backstage. Without the cameras recording the meeting there would be no story. Mike admitted his reason for picking my letter- it was a nice story, but most of all; it was a story people would watch. Without the story Mike would have to pull the plug on the entire meeting.

I was disappointed. I never thought Barry would turn us down. I agreed with Mike. I could transfer from my chair, but why should I? Being in a wheelchair had nothing to do with this story, my relationship with Liv, or our love for Barry's music.

Even if we didn't meet Barry, at least I would still have my dignity.

All we wanted was to say hello, to let him know how much his music meant to us. We were his fans; the ones who bought his records, who waited in ticket lines for hours, who attended the concerts. We were the fans who wouldn't miss a television show or article in the newspaper, who learned the words to every song, and who ultimately fell in love because of his music.

I felt hurt, foolish and disillusioned. Mike said not to suddenly hate Barry Manilow. After all, it was legal hassles and publicity people whom Mike was dealing with.

I would still love his music. That would never change. But my idolized vision of the man had changed, and I was crushed, although old enough to know better.

Mike felt even worse then I did. He did all he could. We both felt bad for Liv. It was too late to get a refund on her plane ticket. She was coming, story or not, and that still meant more to me then anything. I couldn't wait to see her. I dreaded the thought of calling her to tell her of the plans falling through. It was all a big mistake. I was beginning to regret writing that letter in the first place.

Even if we didn't meet Barry we would have a great weekend together. We would even go to the concert.

Not everyone can meet Barry. I was lucky enough to meet him at the bookstore. I tried not to feel bitter. But I wanted Liv to meet him too. She deserved it, after everything we had been through.

Now I was prepared to hurriedly rearrange many of the details at the last minute: how to pick up Liv at the airport, how she would get back, things I had to quickly work out.

My faith in many things had been shaken but I still prayed for a miracle, convinced something would happen, if only we believed.

Mike called back, just when things looked the darkest. Barry's people were still saying no to the television cameras backstage to film the meeting, however a compromise was in the works. Barry DID want to meet us after all, and he claimed to remember me from the bookstore. My faith was rewarded! They reached a compromise on Wednesday. Did the international peace talks cause so much complication?

The station would be allowed to film the first three songs of the show but they still wouldn't allow cameras backstage. Mike said they could work around that. Although filming the actual meeting would have been terrific, Mike wanted our dream to come true, especially after the hassles all week.

Mike called Liv to check on her arrival time and to get some background for the story. She was excited, as I was. I was still confused about the initial resistance but I imagined it was a legal matter, and I was just happy that everything was settled.

I learned a lot that week. Reality was a real slap in the face. I learned a little bit about celebrities, legal technicalities and egos.

I also learned there were still some truly nice, caring people around, like Mike, who risked his reputation by sticking up for us all week against some pretty powerful people.

As I woke on Friday morning I imagined the day ahead. Seeing Liv again would be unbelievable. The rest of the day promised to be as crazy as the roller coaster week we had just gone through.

Our wish was finally coming true. Liv and I would meet the guy who brought us together- Barry Manilow.

Dressed in a chocolate brown suit and tie, I waited with Mom for Mike and the television crew to arrive. It was ten o'clock in the morning, a bright, sunny crisp day. Butterflies soared in my stomach.

Suddenly a huge white stretch limo pulled into our driveway. The neighbors had to think someone had died.

I finally met the famous Mike in person. I knew him so well from his reports on television, a guy of medium height and weight, with brown, curly hair and a friendly smile. I got to know him even better from our frequent phone conversations over the week.

I thanked him for everything. It had been a week that was rough on the nerves and emotions. The real story was just beginning.

With Mike was his cameraman, John, a short fellow with dark hair and a moustache, and R.J. the limo driver, an older guy with silver hair and a slight British accent.

I climbed into the backseat of the gigantic limo, waving bye to Mom, who was equally stunned. She would drive down to the shore later with my sister, aunt and uncle. Liv and I would return home with my family.

As the crew put the wheelchair in the trunk (a limo has a trunk?), I looked around in wonder, my first time in a limo. The seats (a long, semi-circle couch) were red crushed velvet. There were lights and buttons everywhere. A small TV, a car phone even a bar was around me. The front seat seemed miles away.

I felt like a king, but very out of place. Maybe a little embarrassed? I wasn't used to such luxury. Who knows if I would ever be in a limo again?

The limo was a surprise. We were riding in style, thanks to the station.

Even Mike was amazed. I thought he would be used to limos, but he even commented on the size of the car. He took off his shoes, loosened his tie and lit up a cigarette. "This isn't too bad to take, is it?" he smiled.

Mike wanted to take a few shots of where I worked to set up the story I called work to get their approval, and they said sure, come on over.

On the way I looked out the stained-glass windows, smiling at the expressions of the other drivers who were squinting to see who was inside. Riding in a limo- through my hometown- the stuff dreams are made of!

When we arrived at work the publicity people were taking pictures. Mike set up the camera and had me wheel in the office as the film rolled. Co-workers buzzed by, wondering what was happening.

I blew a couple of lines, as Mike asked what my wish was on camera. "My wish is for me and my fiancée to see Barry Manilow in concert and meet him after the show."

Simple enough right? My mouth was as dry as a desert and my hands were sweaty. I earned a newfound respect for actors.

Back on the road, we stopped in nearby Valley Forge. I learned some "inside" tricks of pulling a report together as they left the cameraman off a few times in the freezing cold to take some shots of the passing limo.

By that time we were pressing for time, so we headed for New York, via the Pennsylvania Turnpike. We relaxed and talked while Mike related some local show biz gossip.

Then came the part I dreaded most of all: the interview. We had nearly three hours to go before Kennedy Airport, so there was plenty of time for questions.

Mike asked why I wrote to "Three Wishes". I explained on camera about my relationship with Liv, how we met, and the connection with Manilow's music. I also mentioned my childhood, the broken bones and hospital stays.

He asked if I knew any Norwegian. I repeated the first phrase I could think of: Jeg elsker deg"- "I love you". I didn't think they would use that part in the final report.

I couldn't blame Barry for disliking cameras. If I could have crawled into a cozy corner with Liv, quietly watching the show, then ease backstage and say hello to Barry, that would have been fine with me. No lights, no camera, no action- but also no story.

To my surprise I wasn't as nervous as I thought. I even remembered not to look directly into the camera. If I mumbled or drew a blank we could always start again.

Although Mike would end up shooting a couple of reels of film, everything would be chopped to a mere five minutes. The best, and thankfully the worst of me, may end up on the cutting room floor.

As Mike composed the story in a notebook, trying to make sense of my interview, I quietly gazed out the window. We glided into New Jersey, then New York. We were getting closer to JFK- and Liv.

I thought of her, flying to the States, thinking how crazy she must think the whole story was, thinking how much I loved her, and how far we had come from just being pen pals.

We arrived at the airport at 1:30, just in time to meet Liv. We waited outside of customs, the crew getting permission to film Liv and my reaction when she emerged from customs. Passersby and travelers watched with curiosity.

" Is that her?" Mike yelled, as another blond came out of customs.

"No," I assured, promising to give him the sign when Liv appeared. They didn't want to miss the moment we reunited, and they only had one chance to get it.

"There she is!" I blurted out, seeing Liv smile. She looked just as gorgeous as ever, wearing a brown coat. It was the first time we met in the winter. She carried a small suitcase, just enough for the weekend.

"Go!" Mike snapped to the cameraman.

"Hi!" Liv said, hugging me. "Good to see you!"

"You look great!" I said, smiling in return. For a fleeting moment we forgot the camera was there. Only for a moment.

Introductions were quickly passed around, and before we knew it, we were on the road again, heading for Atlantic City.

Liv looked fantastic, especially after the long eight-hour flight/ She couldn't get over the limo, the cameras, and just the fact this was all true. She knew there would be cameras and publicity but until it actually hit her, she didn't realize the extent of what was happening. She was usually shy, so this extra attention took some getting used to.

Mike and the crew stopped for a quick bite to eat along the turnpike. Liv had eaten on the plane, and I was too hyper to be hungry, so we waited in the limo for the crew.

It gave us a few moments to finally be alone and greet each other properly. It would be the only chance to be alone all day. We talked about the week behind us, the night ahead and just how unbelievable this whole idea was.

Liv was tired from the journey but excited about meeting Barry later that evening. Meeting Barry? It had a nice ring to it. It still seemed like a dream.

Mike did a short interview with Liv as we rode along. His first question was why travel over 6,000 miles to meet Barry?

"First of all, I wanted to see Greg again, " she said sweetly. (I blushed profusely).

"And this is like an adventure," she continued. "It's the chance of a lifetime."

Halfway down the turnpike our lone camera died. So Mike stopped at a phone booth, calling the station back in Philadelphia, arranging for both another camera and a relief guy for the exhausted cameraman. They would meet us at a predetermined phone booth just outside of Atlantic City.

Mike worried about time, chain-smoking and chewing gum constantly. Tough work, this television business. A lot of pressure. "But I love it, " Mike declared, lighting up again.

He was forming the story and the rest of the evening in his mind. "Manilow music in the background as the report begins...Have to do some promos on the Boardwalk... When is the show? Ten-thirty? We will get some shots of you guys being seated in the theatre, if we ever get another camera".

We waited close to an hour for the news van to meet us. By now, twilight was creeping over South Jersey, and the lights from the Atlantic City skyline could be seen across the distant bay.

We finally rode into Atlantic City, the new cameraman, Joe, hanging on top of the news van, filming our limo alongside as we made our glorious entrance into the seaside resort.

As soon as we arrived at the casino we were treated like royalty. The head of the casino's entertainment and publicity department, a young, blonde woman pleasantly greeted us at the door. She apologized for any inconveniences earlier in the week. She also surprised us by exchanging our tickets for seats near the front of the stage!

After that, Barry's crew- Marc, Susan, his manager, couldn't do enough for us. They said that Barry couldn't wait to meet us after the show.

Mike was perplexed. Why weren't they this nice earlier in the week? Maybe they sensed the negative reaction and bad publicity, which Mike hinted, might grow if the story wasn't done? Maybe they wanted to make amends, thinking it wasn't such a bad story after all. Or maybe Barry finally found out what was really going on and cracked the whip.

Mike didn't want to damper our evening, so he went along with it, still mumbling that he "never had the same problems with Julio Iglesis".

Whatever had happened, we were VIPs for an evening. Mike was happy that everything worked out. Despite the tremendous amount of red tape to put the story together, this was more then just another story to him. He was determined to see justice served, like a mission now.

Mike made one last plea to have the cameras go backstage during the climatic meeting, but the answer was still no. He didn't want to press his luck, so he smiled, saying to the road manager, "Can't blame me for trying, can you?"

The road manager wasn't amused.

It was Friday evening, around 8:00, and the casino and lobby was bustling with people, most dressed to kill. There were elderly ladies carrying cups filled with silver, heading for the clanking slot machines. Casino bosses strolled the floors, as did winners and losers. Waitresses in short skirts sprinted across the plush red carpet, balancing trays filled with drinks.

Manilow fans abounded everywhere, their identity known by very familiar t-shirts bearing Barry's likeness. There was noise and glitter everywhere, with roars of guys at the crap tables mixed with squeals of Manilow fans greeting each other.

After dinner we filmed the promotional spots, throwing on some coats and heading out to the deserted boardwalk. It was very quiet, the dark, sparkling ocean calm, compared to the racket in the casino. It was cold too. Light snowflakes fell as we did the commercial.

Mike and Liv stood behind me as Mike announced, "Liv, Greg and I are going inside to get a bit to eat. We'll tell you all about the big meeting with Barry Manilow tomorrow night on Eyewitness News. This is "Three Wishes" for you..."

Reality television at its best!

127

Tomorrow night? Mike was planning for this report to be in two parts, the first part focusing on the reunion with Liv, the second part detailing what happened in Atlantic City.

The actual report wouldn't air until a month later. So, there would be not one, but two nights of us on the news. Could the Delaware Valley stand it?

They took us through the kitchen and backstage in order to reach our seats in the theatre, to avoid the steps. As we watched the theatre fill with fans, Mike departed to direct the action in the back, where the camera was located to catch the first part of the show. He left us with some final instructions.

"Since we can't take the camera backstage, I'm going to count on you to give me a detailed account of everything that goes on."

Mike planned to interview us after meeting Barry. All he said, aside from remembering everything that Barry would say, was to look excited for the cameras. No trouble there, Mike.

A last minute stroke of brilliance overtook Mike. He gave me his camera (the regular kind), saying with a wink, "We can't take our cameras back there- but you can."

Liv was taking her camera. I took Mike's. If questioned, say it was mine. If given the chance, take as many pictures as possible. Mike was cooking up a scheme to somehow work these photos into the story.

I felt like James Bond. I would do my best.

Liv and I sat at a small table on the extreme right of the stage. The high rollers and fan club members filled the front rows, and the entire theatre was sold out.

I remembered the first time I saw Barry in concert, in that very same theatre. It was back in 1981, and my seat was as far back as you can get- Row Z. Still, I had a terrific time, and experienced my first exciting Manilow concert, despite the distance.

I had come a long way from Row Z.

For Liv, it was the first time she would see Barry live in five years. She also came a long way from that ticket line in Oslo back in 1983. She really did come a long way since- 6,000 miles, to be exact.

Since those first concerts we had come a long way- together. Now, I held Liv's hand as the lights dimmed and the music played. The speakers blared, the crowd screamed, and everyone stood.

I looked at Liv. Here it was, our dream come true- seeing Barry, together at last!

Barry opened the show in the middle of the audience, singing the exciting "I'm Your Man", while kissing female fans and shaking hands on his way to the stage.

When finally in view, Barry was wearing a dark pinstriped suit, which was in danger of being ripped off his body by over-zealous fans in the aisles.

On stage (and still in one piece), he swung into songs from his latest album, "Swing Street", as the crowd cheered, clapped and sang along.

Then came those sweet, marshmallow ballads, songs like "Weekend In New England" and "Mandy." During "Can't Smile Without You" Liv was too shy to raise her hand to sing with Barry. Maybe she would never get on stage, but until then she would just have to be content with going backstage.

Barry did all of our favorites. The show's finale, and the highlight of the ninety-minute performance, was Barry's "Gonzo Hits" melody- over twenty songs in a row, lasting nearly a half-an-hour non-stop. Everything from "Tryin' To Get The Feeling" to "It's A Miracle" to our sentimental favorite, "Somewhere Down The Road", the song which just about summed up our relationship.

The emotional, powerful climax was "I Write The Songs", wrapping up his brilliant package of hits, just for his fans.

The crowd stood for nearly five minutes afterwards, not only for the terrific performance, but also for all the years.

Barry did a rousing encore of "I'm Your Man" to end the show. We had forgotten about the cameras. We cheered wildly until the curtain closed.

As the crowd buzzed, slowly filing out of the theatre, Liv glanced at me, both of us exhausted and thrilled. What did we think? Fantastic!

The concert alone would have been enough. But we still had one little thing to take care of yet- meeting Barry.

The excitement and adrenaline were flowing. Susan came over and talked, saying she would escort us backstage in a few moments to see Barry. We chatted for a few minutes, and then she asked, to my surprise, if Mike had given us a camera to take backstage. Was she reading my mind?

"No," I answered quickly. I was never good at lying, always with the thought that honesty was best. But darned if it didn't work!

With my old pals, the butterflies, soaring around my stomach, we followed Susan through a dark corridor to a gray, narrow hallway, where we waited against a concrete wall with several other people nearby. Some were holding copies of Barry's book, all dressed very nicely.

Barry would emerge from the dressing room any moment now. This was it. I looked up at Liv, who said she was fine. It was close to midnight. She had been up for twenty-seven straight hours. As always, she looked beautiful.

What was she thinking just then? Maybe she was remembering our first letters, recalling everything we had gone through since. As on cue, our eyes met, and we blew each other a kiss.

I love you-that's what we were thinking.

What a special girl. I was so lucky to have found her.

Luck...Destiny...Fate. Along with a lot of love. If the fan club had not matched us together, .if we never met, .if Mike never picked my letter. Imagine all the fans that would give their right arm to be where we were!

Just then, Marc came over to greet us. He was dressed in a gray suit and tie. I introduced him to Liv, and he was amazed she had traveled all the way from Norway-that same day- just for the show.

As we were talking, I looked up and there was Barry Manilow, a few feet away, signing some books. He wore a beautiful royal blue sweater and dark slacks. He held a half-full champagne glass.

He noticed us and said a cheerful "Hi!" walking over, asking Marc to remove the rope railing that separated us.

There we were- our wish come true- Liv Barry- and me face-to-face-to-face!

Just like the bookstore, everything I had planned on saying went out the window. Shaking hands, I asked Barry if he remembered me.

"Sure," he said. "How could I forget?"

Barry finally met Liv, mentioning that Oslo was one of his favorite places to play. He remembered the lovely sculpture park in the middle of the city, which he visited in 1983 (Liv always wanted to show me that same park).

Like everyone else, Barry was surprised at Liv's durability, a Trans-Atlantic flight, the ride to Atlantic City, the concert, then and a return trip to Norway on Monday. She was a loyal fan.

The visit was nice. We just hung around, very informally, chatting as though we were old friends. Barry was very down-to-earth and friendly, easy with a laugh and a joke.

"So, when's the wedding?" he asked.

I babbled something about "sometime soon". As Mike kidded later, we should have invited Barry to the wedding right then, but he probably wouldn't allow cameras there either.

We told Barry how much we loved his music. I showed him the original letter that the fan club sent me. Marc read it aloud after Barry held it up to the light, squinting without his glasses.

Finally, Barry asked if there was anything we wanted him to do-autographs?

Once again, Liv saved the day. "We would love to take a picture with you!" she eagerly asked.

"Sure," he said, smiling (whatever happened to the no camera policy?).

So, with Barry on the right, smilingly brightly, Liv in the middle, very ecstatic, and yours truly on the left, grinning sheepishly, Marc snapped the shot.

"Let's take one more, just to make sure we got it," Marc suggested.

So we did. A moment that would live forever.

We said our farewells, thanking everyone. Barry wished us good luck in the future. He wished Liv a safe trip home, and he would "see us again sometime."

It happened so fast, and it was over. We could have talked all night. There were so many things we could have asked him. We appreciated the time we did spend with Barry. Everything wouldn't sink in until later.

When we emerged into the theatre once more, Mike, and the rolling camera, greeted us.

What were our reactions? "Great! He was very nice." Liv felt "shaky" but said that everything was "worth it."

Mike asked what Manilow said. We tried to recall everything the best we could. We forgot that millions of people would eventually see the report. I certainly forgot most of the conversation (short-term memory loss). We were still in a fog.

Off-camera, Mike was especially happy that we got two pictures.

Liv was a bit hesitant about giving up her film (the photos were on her camera, not Mike's). I couldn't blame her for being worried. Those pictures were our proof, worth their weight in gold, at least to us.

Mike promised to develop the film and send everything-pictures and negatives- back as soon as possible.

My family was waiting for us for the trip back home. It was time to say goodbye. Liv gave Mike a crystal knick-knack that she bought in Oslo. He was speechless, glad that our dream had come true.

We thanked Mike and the crew. He would keep in touch, letting us know the date when our report would be shown on the news. After all the calls the last few weeks, and after meeting him in person, I was sorry he would disappear from my life, just as suddenly as he had appeared.

As we waved, he looked back and shouted, "Let me know the wedding date. Maybe we can do a future story!"

We arrived home close to 3:00am. Liv was exhausted, but we still found time to hold each other in my room and dream about our incredible day. What a wonderful experience, something we would always cherish for the rest of our lives.

We weren't hams, but we agreed, the cameras weren't so bad after all. However, if they ever did decide to make a movie about our relationship, someone else could go right ahead and play us, thank you.

Thinking back, we realized why Barry might have resisted the cameras so much. Our meeting was meant to be very private and special. Barry didn't need publicity to do something nice.

Liv thought Barry looked shorter in person, odd because I imagined him to be taller at the bookstore.

Why didn't she give him a big hug and kiss when she had the chance? Well, she didn't want to seem like a wild, fanatical fan.

Of course, Liv was determined never to wash the sweater she was wearing again (Gasp! Barry touched it!).

The rest of the weekend was just for us. Like our visit with Barry, the weekend went too quickly. On Saturday we recuperated from Friday, just catching up on old times. On Sunday we had a family dinner (spaghetti, of course, our favorite) and watched old Manilow tapes on the VCR, sparking old memories. They reminded us that all three of us had come a long way.

By Monday it was time for Liv to leave. Instead of our time together growing longer, it was shrinking, from two months, then two weeks, and now three days.

On the final day a local newspaper reporter stopped by to do an interview and take a nice, cozy photo in my living room. The article would hit the front page of our newspaper later in the week.

More publicity! At least in Norway, Liv was still unknown. Here in America, she would soon be famous. I think in that way, she was glad to be going home.

I rented a limo (a smaller one this time) to take us to New York. More tearful good-byes until the upcoming summer.

The backseat of the limo seemed so lonely and empty on the way home. Every time Liv left, she took a piece of my heart with her. For some strange reason the movie "Brigadoon" stuck in my mind on my way home. It was a musical fantasy about an American who stumbles upon a magical Scottish village that appears only one day each century. The American guy falls in love with a Scottish lass who resides in the village. It is an ill-fated romance, despite their deep love for each other.

The village vanishes after a day, and the heart-broken American returns to New York. His friends tell him to forget his long-lost love, but he can't. She is constantly on his mind and in his heart.

So, he leaves his girlfriend, his job, his friends, his entire former life, and returns to Brigadoon to find his true love. Through a miracle, because of their undying love, they are reunited-forever.

That movie reminded me of my relationship with Liv. So distant in miles yet so close to the heart. My friends had also told me to forget her and that it wouldn't work out. But my thoughts always drifted back to Liv. Pretty soon my friends were convinced that it just might work out after all.

More then just the film, I recalled the moral of Brigadoon: if the love is strong enough, anything is possible. Our love seemed strong enough. We did believe in each other, and we knew that someday we would never have to say goodbye again.

Our relationship was just as magical. Our love would also survive time, distance and fate.

Along with the tears, there were smiles and fond memories. What a weekend it was! The summer was only five months away. Seeing Liv again couldn't come too soon.

A week after Liv left, our article appeared on the front page. There we were, arm in arm, all smiles. A nice article accompanied the photo. I sent the Liv the article, after buying out all the newspapers I could find.

For a little while I was somewhat of a local hero. I received cards of congratulations and phone calls from well wishers. Everyone wanted to meet Liv, asking when she was coming back. The most popular question was "When are you getting married?"

I really didn't know. We were just taking it one day at a time. We planned to meet again during the upcoming summer, then possibly Liv would move over for good that autumn. Funny, before no one took our relationship seriously. Now, everyone was asking when we would tie the knot.

Mike returned our pictures and there we were again, next to Barry Manilow. It really did happen! I rushed the photos to Liv, who made more copies and sent them back. I was wondering what the reaction was like in Norway.

The publicity from the newspaper article was nothing compared to the television special. It aired during the first weekend in April, Easter weekend.

Mike let me know the day before, and I tried to call as many friends and relatives as I could. Still, I was a bit embarrassed by the fuss, and even reluctant to see myself on the screen. I was happy about the whole thing, yet didn't know what to expect.

Near 11:00 pm, my VCR ready to roll, I checked everything again and again so I wouldn't mess up the taping. I wanted Liv to see it someday, and even if I missed it, Tom, Mark, Pat, Phyllis and a host of other family members were taping it, just in case.

Talk about nerve-wracking! It was two months between meeting Barry and the report airing. The excitement had been building all this time, and now, here it was- our story- in living color, the Delaware Valley's answer to prince Charles and Princess Diana (well, sort of).

Before the news they ran the promo. There I was, looking cold on the boardwalk, with Liv and Mike standing behind me, while the anchorman said "And tonight on "Three Wishes", Mike brings you a story about a boy from Phoenixville and a girl from Norway, and their dream come true."

Suddenly reality hit me. Me? On the news? No, it had to be another Smith. Smith is a common name.

Meeting Barry Manilow- the superstar? The story of Liv, and me detailed on the air?

Mom and I watched, and about midway through the news they finally ran our three-minute segment.

"This is more then just two pen pals meeting," Mike said on the tape. "It's a love story."

I blushed, afraid to look at the screen.

The initial shot of me, wheeling in the office at work, while Mike set up the story. And there I was, wishing my wish then the screen- and my face- dissolved into Barry singing the first song of the show.

They showed me riding in the huge white limo, looking a little like Donald Trump, explaining to Mike what Manilow's music meant to me, and how I felt about Liv. He even left in the part where I said, "I love you" in Norwegian.

The memories returned as I watched us nearing Kennedy Airport, while the Manilow song "Brooklyn Blues" played in the background. There was Liv, hugging me as we were reunited.

They showed a bit of Liv's interview as we rode to Atlantic City, especially when she said the main reason for traveling so far was to see me again. And finally, there we were on the Boardwalk, freezing as Mike closed with, "And we'll tell you all about the meeting with Barry Manilow tomorrow night."

Same time, same station.

Immediately the phone started ringing. I imagined people over all Philly, Jersey, Delaware talking about us, especially Manilow fans. How many thousands-or millions- watched it? I tried not to think of the possibilities.

The entire area was getting to share in an old-fashioned love story, the kind they don't make anymore.

Judging from the phone calls, it seemed as though the station had high ratings that night. I was hearing from old friends and relatives I hadn't heard from in years. It was like winning the lottery. Everyone looked forward to part two the following night.

The second part began by recapping the previous nights; segment. Next we were at the concert, smiling and having a good time, while Barry danced with the audience.

For all of those people who thought they were going to see Liv and I actually meet Barry, they were disappointed. Mike got around that by saying Barry wouldn't allow cameras backstage because he considered it a "personal moment."

There we were again, with our reactions after the show. I looked pretty nervous as I tried to remember our conversation with Manilow.

The final shot of the report was a nice touch: our famous photo with Barry, taken by Marc, as "Looks Like We Made It" played over the fading scene.

The report was intelligent and sensitive, focusing on the theme of that day- our love for each other.

I forgot about the red tape leading up to that day and the hectic schedule of the day itself. Instead, I remembered how magical the experience was. And how lucky I was to share it with the most special person in the world. I thanked Mike for making it possible.

The following week was almost as unbelievable. Strangers came up to me on the street or in the elevator at work, asking "Aren't you the guy who was on the news?" Other fans wrote to the fan club, asking how they could contact me. One woman found out where I worked and came in just to say hello. My co-workers went out oft heir way to let me know they had seen the special and were happy for us, and wished us luck.

It was all so perfect. I heard from fan clubs around the area, and even one from Louisiana, asking me to join their club. The videotape of the report was floating around the country, and a club from Florida showed it during one of their monthly meetings. Vicki and Chris were some of the happiest fans, because we were good friends.

The question remained- when are you getting married? I imagined having to rent the Spectrum in Philadelphia for the reception. I was happy so many people cared.

Within a few weeks it was back to "Greg who?" I enjoyed my brush with fame while it lasted, but was glad to get back to my "Greg who" status.

It was a happy time in my life, a time I needed for the memories, as difficult times approached in very surprising fashion.

8. LIFE WILL GO ON

Barry was coming back to the area in August, this time bringing his full concert show to the beautiful Mann Music Center, an outdoor theatre outside of Philadelphia. I couldn't wait to get tickets, hoping Liv would be able to come over.

There was one hitch: a local radio station bought out all of the tickets-about 10,000, in a promotional stunt. The tickets would be given away within the next several weeks. I had to qualify first by sending in the contest coupon. Every hour the station would announce several names. If your name was called, you had a short time to call back and claim the free tickets.

In other words, if I wanted to see Manilow this time, I would have to get lucky.

I listened to the radio every waking moment, hoping my name would be called. Could I get to the phone in time? What if my name was picked while I was at work?

It was frustrating because many fans never bothered to call back for their tickets. Some listeners weren't real Manilow fans, at least not as devoted as Vicki and me. Many called because the tickets were free. Here I was, staying up all night, carrying a radio with me constantly, and dying to hear my name, but as the weeks went by, still no luck. I heard a lot of "Smiths" but not the right one.

It was Barry's only appearance in Philly in four years, and it seemed a shame that many of his loyal fans would be shut out of the concert by a stupid contest.

How depressing it would be- Barry so close to home, with Liv possibly here, and not able to get two tickets! All we needed was two tickets!

When all seemed lost, at 2:00 am one morning, as I was dozing off, I vaguely heard my name being announced. At first I thought I was dreaming, then my eyes flew open and I grabbed the phone.

The line was busy. Would I ever get through? I finally did, giving my name and code number, hoping it wasn't a mistake.

I won! Two tickets were winging their way to my mailbox.

So, I had a pair of tickets, and I was happy. Then a friend at work, who also won tickets, but who wasn't a Manilow fan (What?), gave me her tickets. Now I had four.

Then, in a last-minute stunt, the radio station started giving away tickets at local shopping malls. I went to one of the giveaways, and what a circus! Hundreds and hundreds of fans, lined up through out the mall. I saw many familiar faces, and I was nearly caught in a wild stampede when the location of the actual giveaway was switched to across the mall.

I picked up two more tickets. Now I had six.

I tried to help some devoted fans that were shutout. Vicki got her tickets. By hook or by crook, Manilow fans got their tickets somehow. Some went from mall to mall; some stayed up and listened to the radio all night long, listening in shifts; some traded or bartered for seats; others took out ads in the newspaper.

With Barry's ticket one of the hottest of the summer, it reminded me of the good old days. Although Barry's shows continued to sell out, even through the years when his popularity supposedly declined, this summer was still exciting, like the times when you couldn't turn on the radio without hearing a Manilow song somewhere .His music never really left. It was always there- in elevators, restaurants, and piano bars- and still on the radio.

I could have scalped my tickets for at least $300, but I wasn't going to miss seeing Barry again, especially with Liv. The only question was if Liv could make it over.

Liv did make it, her fourth visit to the States, incredible when I recalled how long we waited for her very first visit. For the first time I couldn't meet her at the airport, so Liv caught the airport van to nearby King of Prussia, where we would pick her up.

Liv said not to worry. She would call me at the airport before boarding the van. But, as I waited at home, there was still no word from her. Was she still in customs? Did she make the early van, not having a chance to call? Was her plane delayed? Or was it something worse?

I longed to hear her voice again, praying that she was safe. Each time the phone rang I grabbed it on the first ring, each time disappointed. I felt so helpless.

As the hours passed I grew sorrier that I wasn't at the airport to meet her. If anything ever happened to her, I would never forgive myself.

The phone suddenly rang, nearly giving me a heart attack. It was Liv!

If there were any way of crawling through the phone to her, I would have. Hearing her voice made me appreciate her like never before.

Liv's plane did arrive late. Quickly through customs, she barely had enough time to race to another terminal to catch the early van. She was sorry she couldn't call, knowing how I worried.

"Who me? Worry?" I gulped.

We had our outings and our quiet times, only together for two weeks again. At times Liv seemed strangely distant, very unlike her. We still loved each other, but decisions needed to be made and the pressure was growing. Our time was still special, but nothing could compare to that magical first summer. Was the reality of our relationship finally hitting home?

Even so, her kiss let me know that everything would work out. In her love I had no doubt.

We had a basic plan, waiting so long for happiness. Our problem was trying to figure out how to stay on the same continent together.

For the first time during that visit, Liv saw our "Three Wishes" video, hiding her face with a pillow at times. We also began the long process of applying for a "fiancée petition", a special visa that would allow Liv to work and live in the States- if she married an American within a certain amount of time (guess who?).

We didn't set an official wedding date yet. We had to make sure Liv would get her special visa. To apply, we had to fill out countless forms, while gathering birth certificates and Identification photos. It was a lot of work, but worthwhile in the end.

We talked more seriously about issues involving our relationship, such as where we would live (America-at Mom's until we saved enough money and got an apartment), Children was another subject. Would my physical condition enter into having kids? After all the time we spent in baby departments at the mall, I knew Liv wanted children someday, and I knew she would be a great mother.

I did some research on Osteogenisis Imperfecti. It is a genetic disorder, and there would be no assurance it couldn't be passed on to my kids. But then again, we couldn't live in fear.

We shared another fantastic Manilow concert together on a warm, starry evening. We didn't bump into Barry this time, but it didn't matter.

For some reason I had a feeling through out her visit that I would never see her again. Call it a feeling in my soul. The memories kept me hopeful, the future looked bright, when each day would be special, not just a summer. Yet I still had this feeling, which I couldn't explain.

We said, "I'll see you" as we parted, and I wondered how many more times I could let her go.

Liv couldn't afford a phone in her new apartment yet, so I couldn't call her as often as before. I felt so out of touch. She liked her new job and new life as a lawyer in Oslo. Our letters continued, as did our plans. Her visa was due any day now. The gigantic ocean, the mountain of red tape, and the vast distance of time, the lingering doubts and fears- we were still certain that nothing could stop us.

Then it happened so suddenly. First, my job. The county didn't want to pick up the tab anymore for my transportation. I was surprised it lasted as long as it did. They liked me, liked my work, but my supervisor laid down the law. Either I had to find another mode of transportation, a car-pool, a bus, or pay for the cab ride myself each day. Or I had to finally learn to drive. The other options were, resign or termination.

I really liked the job, and felt comfortable there, after an initial rocky start. But I couldn't afford to pay the expensive cab ride back and forth to work each day. What would be the use of working, if most of my salary would go to transportation alone?

I was still afraid to drive. I knew it was the answer, but I just couldn't do it. I couldn't find anyone to car-pool with. No one lived near Phoenixville, and people were not willing to go a few miles out of their way, as Laurie had. The bus station was five blocks away from work, and most of the curbs in Norristown at that time were not accessible for a wheel chair. Mom was not feeling well, and I couldn't expect her to be my ride forever.

I didn't want to quit. I didn't want to go back to unemployment, disability benefits, looking for another job. I regretted not accepting the position the local hospital, and when I contacted them about a possible opening I was told that I had my chance. Obviously, there were still hard feelings, which I could understand.

I finally found a job where I could help others in need. All the years of studying to become a social worker, of searching for work, and now I was in danger of losing my job and returning to life before. I felt like a failure.

Reluctantly, I resigned. My co-workers sympathized with my decision, but what could they do? They didn't want to risk losing their jobs. All they could say was "good luck" and encouraged me not to give up, that something good would happen in my life.

Cleaning out my desk was like the end of the world. I gave them two weeks' notice. I was on borrowed time, and was treated as such. I started sending out resumes again. But no matter where I applied, the same problem faced me. Who would hire me now, after I already had transportation problems?

I had sent Liv flowers that week, for no reason, other to say, "I love you". I didn't tell her about my problems at work. I felt something good would happen. As it turned out, I didn't need to tell her.

Usually I couldn't wait to open Liv's letters, but this time I hesitated when I found the envelope on my bed after work. I changed first, staring at the letter. Maybe I was scared because it had taken an unusual length of time answering my last letter. Somehow I felt uneasy, as my worst nightmare came true.

The letter began as always, well, almost. Instead of "Dearest" Greg, it began "Dear" Greg. That is where any similarities to her hundreds of past letters ended. I couldn't believe what I was reading.

Liv was saying goodbye. She was ending our relationship.

It was the hardest letter she ever wrote, or so she claimed. She would have called instead, but tears got in the way. And Norway wasn't exactly close enough to drop by and tell me face-to-face. This was the only way to relate her feelings, as our relationship began- in a letter.

Time and distance had faded her love for me. She just couldn't go through with our plans. There was no one new. I don't think she would've told me anyway, to save my feelings. It was "her fault", and I had been great to her over the years, which made her decision so difficult.

A "little voice" inside her was telling her that marriage was not right, after spending so little time together. She needed time to think- to "find herself". All she could offer now was friendship.

She knew I would feel guilty, angry, cheated and hurt. But as I read on, I felt nothing, too shocked to feel anything.

She wanted to remain friends. I was her best friend ever, helping her to live and love again. She understood if I never wrote back. She closed by writing, "I'm so sorry." And that was that.

I was devastated. In time I might understand, but at that moment I felt empty inside, as if someone close to me had died. I kept asking why. I had lost my best friend too, someone very special to me.

This was Liv saying goodbye, not just any girl. The girl in all my hopes and dreams, the girl I still loved more then anything.

How could I trust anyone again? How could I ever listen to another Manilow song without thinking of her, without crying?

Barry! I remembered our times together, meeting Barry, how we started as pen pals. I felt so sad that our fairy tale had ended.

After five years, why now? I was surprised, but thinking back, I finally noticed the signs. The pressure of the visa, of getting married, of leaving her job, her family, her country. What could I offer her that would outweigh her entire life/?

She had told me all that time, don't worry. She wanted to be with me. We would work it out, no matter what. Our love was too strong, our bond too close, to ever give up. I believed her.

Even through bitterness I could see her point. Our relationship was such a whirlwind, so magical, and at the end, reality set in. She had also worked so hard to build her life-why give it all up on me?

Who knows what was going on in Norway? I never met her family, her friends, which I knew wasn't good. Did they finally convince her that she was making a big mistake? Did she really find someone new, and decided the hassle wasn't worth it? Or was it as simple as, her love for me did lessen as the years went by?

It wasn't her job or the difficult adjustment to another culture that changed her mind. Her feelings had changed. I never thought Liv would stop loving me, or would be dishonest in her feelings and sincerity. I really believed she did love me-at one time- and maybe still loved me. Maybe she just wasn't "in love" with me any more? That was the most difficult of all the broken dreams to accept.

I couldn't eat or sleep or even work, although I went to work, finishing out my time. Losing my job, the pressure of driving, now losing Liv- nothing seemed to matter without Liv.

I almost lost it when I heard "Somewhere Down The Road" over the radio at work. I managed to hold up. Only at night did my defenses lower. I started dreaming about Liv, always the same vivid nightmare. I went to Norway, like a knight in shining armor, frantically searching the streets of Oslo in vain for her, only to wake up in a cold sweat, crying.

Only this wasn't a dream. I did lose Liv.

Liv seemed everywhere. A Norwegian won the New York City Marathon. The Winter Olympics were being planned for Norway. Miss Norway became Miss Universe. There were still Norwegian stickers around my house. The sweater she knitted for me still hung in my closet. I couldn't get away from it.

When I went out with friends to forget, I saw her wherever I looked- our favorite restaurant, the mall, and the movies. Even another Manilow concert wasn't the same.

My friends did their best to encourage me, saying that I was special, that maybe it happened for the best, that someone new would come along. Who needed Liv anyway?

"When's the wedding?" That same question haunted me. Liv and Greg- couldn't think of one without the other.

As the weeks drifted by my feelings changed from depression to bitterness. How could she throw everything away? Did she just use me? Did she ever really love me?

If only things were different. If I could go to Norway, see her and, talk to her. Could she look me in the eyes, as she did so many times with love, and say goodbye?

I had to let go sooner or later. I wasn't exactly a popular guy in the dating scene, so I spent lonelier Friday and Saturday nights at home, watching television, back to where I was before. It seemed like nothing had changed in all those years.

I called some female friends from back in college, and we went out a few times. But they had moved on too, and it just wasn't the same. I still cared for Liv, and until I closed the door on that relationship, it wasn't fair to try and open another door- not fair to me or to the next innocent person.

There was no one like her, and I was afraid there would never be anyone like her again. It was fun while it lasted.

I was determined not to give up. Thoughts of traveling to Norway still tortured me. Braving the cold and distance, flying so far, waiting outside her apartment in the snow with flowers in hand, she would run into my arms, her heart melting like old times, and we would be together always, living happily ever after, just like in the movies.

The truth was that I was afraid to accept the truth. I had built this image of Liv in my mind, of what I wanted her to be like, not what she really was, and now I couldn't face the fact that she didn't love me anymore.

There were thoughts of trashing all remembrances of Liv, throwing away her many cards and letters and gifts, and starting over.

But I still, deep in my heart, believed she loved me, if not then, but once. And I had to appreciate those special memories. At least she was mine, if only for a short time.

Months passed without Liv in my life. I missed her letters. I wondered if I should call her in Larvik over the holidays. If she needed time to think, maybe it was better to drift away. I also needed time to mend a broken heart.

I would always be there, if she needed me. I couldn't suddenly forget her. Maybe she would miss me someday, and change her mind? Or maybe the memories would fade away as the years disappeared.

All I had left were those memories. Barry's music meant more to me then ever. The music made me cry, but also made me think of her, even though I tried not to, and I smiled, remembering the good times we had together. Songs like "I Made It Through The Rain", "Life Will Go On," and "Please Don't Be Scared" gave me hope, that everything would be all right.

I thought of her each day, as life went on, wondering if she was thinking of me.

Then, in a total surprise, I received a card from her the following spring. She had gotten a copy of our video, and the memories returned. She still wanted to be friends. She offered the option of becoming pen pals again. I guess she missed my letters too.

My foolish pride kept me from writing back. We would go years before connecting again. Much would happen during that time, enough to keep me busy, but even through the years, I would never forget Liv.

After more months of unemployment, of trying to get back on disability, of frustration and hopelessness, finally I caught a break.

I had always worked at the Manor, the nursing home in Phoenixville where I first started volunteering some fifteen years earlier. I worked as a volunteer, as well as some part-time work, helping out in Social Services and Activities, and I also did one of my college internships there, so the staff and especially the Administrator, Mrs. Alfgren, knew me very well.

I was still out of work when I attended the annual Volunteer Luncheon in May of 1990. Mrs. Alfgren, a very short lady, with curly gray hair and a nice smile, came over to me before the luncheon began, asking how I was doing. She was always a nice lady, and actually had started at the nursing home about the same time I started volunteering.

She squinted her eyes and crinkled her nose in that funny way she did when she was thinking. She asked to see me after the luncheon.

The current social worker, Adrienne, was going to have a baby. They needed someone to fill in for six months, until she came back. It wouldn't be a permanent position, as they could only afford one social worker on staff, but at least it would be experience and a job.

Mrs. Afgren knew I didn't have the experience. But I'll never forget her because she gave me a chance. She knew what I lacked in nursing home experience, although I had been a part of the Manor family since 1979, I made up for in life experience and common sense.

I accepted the job. I would start immediately, orientating with Adrienne, until she left on maternity leave on July 1.

I was so thrilled. Imagine! Returning to where it all started, this time as a social worker-my dream come true.

The weeks of orientation went quickly. Adrienne was easy to work with, young, pretty, intelligent. She had been in the field a while, and knew her stuff. I learned something new every day. Even down the road, as a seasoned social worker, I would continue to learn something new each day. It kept the job interesting and fun. You just never knew whom you would meet next or what kind of case you would have to deal with.

We had a tiny office, but we made do. The residents were very happy when they learned that I would be filling in for Adrienne. They knew me, trusted me, and liked me. I really think my O.I. and the fact that I was an invalid as a kid actually helped me over the years. The residents knew, maybe I could empathize a little about what it was like to be bed-bound, to be in pain, to be ill, to be lonely, to feel frustration when your independence is controlled by others.

After July 1 I was on my own. I admit to being a little scared, but as in my college days, I didn't stop to think-I just did it. There were meetings to attend; care plans and notes to write, documentation and forms to complete. There were residents and families to counsel, which was always my favorite part of the job, being with people. The paperwork was a necessity, but I always thought the key to social work was being with the people, and working hands-on with them.

That's why I tried to continue feeding those residents in need of assistance when I could, even though some days I was so busy I didn't have time to have lunch myself. It was important, because it brought me closer to the residents. I never thought of feeding a resident lunch as demeaning work; I thought of it as important work, enjoyable, and humbling.

I did the best I could and learned quickly. The staff were very kind and helpful, and even when the State surveyors made their annual visit, they took into consideration that I was new, and filling in, although they did comment that I was doing a good job, especially considering the circumstances.

Adrienne had a boy in August. She would call me from time to time, to find out how I was doing; help with any questions or problems. She even brought the baby in to see the staff during the fall. She was an excellent social worker, had been at the Manor for several years, and I knew I was only a fill-in. I was happy to see her, but also felt like I was on borrowed time, but went along with my daily work.

At the end of the year it was planned that Adrienne would return to work after the New Year. I hated to leave, and began to send out resumes again. After six months I had become even more of a fixture at the nursing home, and although admittedly, I wasn't as experienced as Adrienne, I tried hard and seemed to have a done a good job. Adrienne said she would talk to Mrs. Alfgren about "needing an assistant", but she couldn't promise anything. It was up to the corporation. Could she justify needing an assistant? Certainly the work was more then enough for one person to handle. A full caseload was 144 residents. Adrienne could use the help, but would they give her an assistant- and would that person be me?

A few days before the New Year Mrs. Alfgren called me into her office. I thought she was just going to thank me for all I had done, which she did. But to my delight, she offered me the position of Social Service Assistant. I was so happy. Of course I accepted. I loved the work, and it was only a block from home. I wouldn't have to worry about transportation any more. I could wheel back and forth to home and work each day myself.

For the next two years I worked as Adrienne's assistant. I learned a lot. I did whatever was asked of me. My documentation was great. In fact, one of the usually stone-faced State inspectors once commented to me, after an exit interview, that my notes were some the best he had read in the state.

I was there for the residents when they were ill, lonely, dying. I was there when we won the E award from the corporation, an award of excellence, after we received a tremendous survey, and the corporation threw the staff a big banquet, along with bonuses for all. I was also there when the surveys weren't so good, and we all worked so hard to clear any deficiencies that were noted.

Luckily, in all my years at the nursing home, our department never once received a penalty. It spoke volumes for our work, and Adrienne and I worked well as a team.

There was pressure- to clean up any deficiencies in time for the return of the inspectors. There was pressure to fill the beds, always a concern. After all, the nursing home was a business. They were there to provide care, but also to make money, So it was a continuing thing to fill the beds, keep them filled, and Adrienne and I did the Admission process as well as social work. It sure kept us hopping.

I learned that nursing home social work was fast-paced, unexpected and challenging. I was proud of the Manor because it wasn't the old, stereotypical nursing home of the past: a hellhole, where residents are mistreated and abused. Ours was a clean, odor-free, bright and cheerful place. Yes, it was a place where people came to live-and eventually die- long term. But we also had more and more cases of rehabilitation cases, of residents who needed some therapy or strengthening, then could return home. I always thought of the facility as a place to come to live, not the old notion of a place to come to die.

Families were as different as the residents, and many experienced grief, guilt, and feelings of being overwhelmed, sadness. I had families crying at my desk, and my job was to provide comfort, many times just listening, offering a few words of support. Some were angry, and deflected their anger to the staff, some very demanding of the staff, unable to care for their loved one, yet demanding, and rightfully so, excellence in care from the staff.

Many families called for help with clothing, arranging dental appointments, transportation. Most just needed guidance and support even those families who were veterans. The cool thing was many families sought out other families and became friends, a mini-support system, and with our Family Council meetings, we would be another source of support as well.

I always felt for the families because many times, the residents themselves, although suffering pain and illness, may not be aware of the situation. Many had Dementia or Alzheimers disease, some more confused then others. Many could remember events that had occurred in the past, twenty, thirty years ago, but could not tell me what they had for breakfast that morning.

But it was the families were knew what was going on. They were the ones who had to watch Mom decline, remembering life before, now angry that Mom wasn't the same. The families were the ones who struggled each day with visiting, with slowly watching the decline of loved ones, especially those with Dementia, from mere forgetfulness, to being bed-bound and needing total care. It was the families who often heard the line "I took care of you when you were a child", yet felt the guilt and grief when realization hit and they concluded that professional care was needed.

The residents needed the same support and comfort. Who wanted to be in a nursing home? After years of working hard, raising families, vacations, good times, bad times, who would ever think that life would come to nursing home care? Many vowed, making family members promise, never to seek nursing home placement. Depression, anxiety and agitation were often the aftermath of admission. Some were accepting of need for care, many coming from a hospital and unable to return home.

Phoenixville was a very ethnic community. Everyone knew everyone else. So when a resident was admitted to the Manor, often they already knew someone else who was there, a neighbor, a friend, and that helped with adjustment and acceptance.

It was hard to see loved ones past away before you-family and friends. My Mom was going through the same thing- seeing old friends pass away. In a nursing home, it was the same deal. Residents would become good friends, like a community within a community, and would enjoy company, activities and meals together. Hearing that a friend had passed away, seeing a funeral director wheel a covered body down the hall to the elevator and to a waiting hearse, the residents had to ask each other "Am I next?" and naturally they would mourn. It was my job to provide counseling and support.

I just never knew what to expect each day- a case of Dementia, of a broken hip, of a stroke. So many ailments, so many personalities. Families who would be supportive and visited regularly, families who never visited at all. I knew young residents, those in their 20s or 30s, there because of diseases such as Huntington', which most often affects people who are younger. Imagine being 35 and having to spend the rest of your life in a nursing home, where the population was mostly in their 80s and 90s? I could especially feel for these younger residents, some just about the same age as I was.

My typical day would be arriving at eight in the morning, doing my charts and paperwork early, before the residents awoke and before the phones started ringing. We would usually have a morning meeting with Mrs. Alfgren and the other department heads in the morning, then depending on admissions, we would go about our daily duties of counseling care plan meetings plus always being alert for emergency situations, when a social worker was needed. Often these situations occurred when a resident became violent, threatening suicide or harm to the staff or other residents, most of the time the result of Dementia or a mental health issue. Often it would be a matter of gentle counseling, and although I tried to never get in the middle of someone who was extremely violent- I wasn't stupid- most of the time I was able to at least convince a resident to calm down and allow staff to help. I learned about body language, tone of voice, how to approach a Demented resident or an agitated person correctly. It all came with experience and a lot of it was pure common sense, things they couldn't teach in a classroom.

There were also less trivial yet important duties too: breaking up roommate fights was a popular, almost everyday occurrence. One person wanted the heat turned up higher; one wanted the television louder. One just wanted a new roommate, and then it was like a jigsaw puzzle of matching up compatible roommates. The goal was to make everyone happy. With 144 people to work with, that wasn't always easy to do.

There were happy times too, joyous times when celebrations occurred: when residents got well enough to return home: we had one couple who met at the nursing home, fell in love, married, and got their own apartment, and lived very well together for the rest of their lives.

I'll never forget one humorous incident, which again proved that anything could happen each day.

I arrived at work, as usual, at eight in the morning, and even before I could take my jacket off, the nurses on the second floor called my office. They needed me to come down, right away, even before I started to do my paperwork.

Thinking it was an emergency I wheeled down the hall at a brisk speed. When I arrived at the nurses' station, the nurses were giggling. I thought they had lost their minds. They liked to tease me anyway, since I was new, cute and blushed easily.

They related there was a lady down the hall, about 95 years old, which needed some "help". I knew this lady well, as I tried to learn everything I could about all of my residents on the floors I was assigned to cover. They said on this morning, all during breakfast, this particular resident kept mumbling to the aide who was feeding her "I need. I need. I need."

The nurses and aides couldn't figure out what she "needed". They offered everything they could think of: water, a bedpan, getting dressed. She refused everything and just kept mumbling, "I need. I need. I need."

Finally, as breakfast concluded, she suddenly blurted out "I need...sex!"

95 years old. I was surprised but then again, I shouldn't have been as I learned over the years, feelings, and desires, even in older adults, often never subsided. It was a law to give residents' their privacy. So, in this case, the nurses naturally called me.

"Go in and take care of her," they encouraged, laughing.

"They never taught me that at West Chester," I replied, half-joking.

She had calmed down eventually. I wrote something very technical in my notes, something like, "resident very agitated this morning. Social Worker provided support. She is better now."

While I'm on the subject, I worked with the residents and families, but I was always there for the staff too. I learned over the years what special people they truly were. Working in a nursing home is very emotional, hard work, both physically and mentally. It was important to offer support and guidance, an offer of a friendly, listening ear, knowing what they were going through, an acknowledgement of doing a good job. I found the latter to be very important. Often staff, especially supervisors, would be caught up in their own work, and forget to offer encouragement and praise for a job well done. Too many times state surveyors would point out the negatives in nursing home care, as I suppose is their job to help to improve care, but I found it also important for those in charge to offer much encouragement to keep moral high and basically to reward caregivers.

Things like occasional pizza parties, gatherings, or just a mention during a general staff meeting that everyone was doing a good job, meant so much. It meant a lot to me too. It validated that I was indeed doing a good job, and kept me going, even though the tough times.

I admired the doctors and nurses and dietary and maintenance and office workers for their dedication. But I probably admired the nurses' aides the most. They did the dirty work- cleaning and showering residents, transferring and lifting people, doing the basic everyday duties, yet very rarely receiving a thank you, paid very minimal wages, yet their dedication was unwavering. Many of the aides grew close to the residents. It wasn't just a job to those who really cared. And many aides would bring in cookies for the residents, or even take some home for dinner. They were friends, talking during care or down times, often family that residents didn't have, or families who didn't visit.

I admired the aides so much, because for very little reward, they laid their hearts on the line each day. When a favorite resident died it was hard to accept, and it was my job to offer support to staff when a beloved resident passed away. It was a risk, getting emotionally involved with a resident, who more then likely would die eventually someday, sooner then later. But if one didn't become involved, if one didn't care, then one might as well be a robot.

I can't say that most aides merely worked in the nursing home for the wages. Most had to care, because they wanted to help those in need, to be there in the first place.

To me, they were truly the backbone of the facility, and never could receive enough praise for their dedication, their work and especially their caring.

After working with Adrienne for two years as an assistant, Adrienne decided to take another Director's job closer to her home in

Pottstown, PA. I would miss her, because we did work well together and she taught me so much about nursing home social work. I was also afraid I might not get another supervisor who was as cool as she was.

Mrs. Alfgren offered me the position of Director of Social Services. At first I said no. Why? Because I was perfectly happy being an assistant. The Director gets the grief when the State comes by. The Director attends all of those needless meetings. I didn't want to be boss. The extra money was nice, but again, I was happy with my wages and my responsibilities. Plus, even after two years, I guess I wasn't totally confident that I could do the job yet.

I wasn't perfect, but who was?

Mrs. Alfgren took resumes, consulted me, but just couldn't find the right person, one with experience, and a person she felt comfortable with. So she asked me again to accept the position, at least until someone overwhelming came along.

I accepted. I knew what I was in for, but considered that a challenge would keep me on my toes, and growth and more experience would be good for me.

So, for the next six years, I was Social Service Director at the Manor. It was all I could hope for, all I ever wanted, all I dreamed about, thinking way back, when I started as volunteer at the nursing home, during my college days, yearning for the position as I worked at Aging, and during the times I was unemployed.

The work wasn't much different then when I was assistant. I still did counseling, paperwork, whatever I needed to do. But now that I had an assistant, I attended most of the meetings, and I was on the hot seat if my department wasn't up to snuff.

I had numerous assistants over the years, some good, some bad. Most stayed for a while, and either found they liked nursing home social work, but moved on after getting their Masters degree, or they hated it. The action was fast-paced and unexpected, and it surprised some assistants once they got into the work.

Changing assistants was frustrating for me. It would take a few months to really orient someone, then they would leave, and I would have to start all over again. In between assistants, I would do both jobs. There were a lapse of months before someone qualified was hired, and doing two jobs in one became stressful at times. I still loved working with the residents but the paperwork and the pressure was huge at times, especially when the State was lurking.

I had two interns from my old alma mater, West Chester University, during my years. That was nice, because it was a way of giving back to my school, and helping new social workers learn the ropes. I wanted to get them excited about social work, especially social work in a nursing home. I hated to give bad grades, and although I knew it was for their own good, I couldn't give a bad grade to a student. I knew what they were going through, knew a good internship was important towards graduation, and felt if they didn't have a good experience under my supervision. I had failed too.

The first student was really shy and quiet. I was too, when I first started in the field. I had to learn to be a bit more forward and open and aggressive. I recommended this approach to my first student after a few weeks. I knew what it was like to be an intern, afraid to step on toes.

I think my advice worked too well, because within weeks, she was giving me advice. I was new at being a supervisor, and she pointed out to me that, even after she was an intern for several weeks, I was still babying her, giving her advice but not allowing her to make mistakes. Instead of leaving her counsel a resident- alone- I had to be there with her. Well, I really didn't have to be there with her, and that was the point.

I sat back and thought, "Wow, she is right!" So, after that, I let her go, and we had a great internship. We both had learned things from each other.

My second student was very emotional. I'll always admire her spunk, because she was a single mother of two small kids, fresh out of a divorce, trying to make it in school in her early 30s. She was frantic, dropping her kids at day care, coming to her internship crying, stressed out, not only from school but also from her personal life. We would take the first hour of each day just to counsel her.

How could she help residents when she was constantly in tears? She bummed me out. I can imagine how the residents would feel. So we had a heart-to-heart talk, and although I felt for her problems, she had to get herself together. I was kind and sympathized with her trials in life, but would her next boss be so understanding once she started working in the field?

By the end of her nine-month run, she was better. I still worried about her in the field, but she had her life together by graduation, and I hoped her good heart and caring personality would carry her through.

She loved kids, and I was happy to hear from her a few months after graduation. She still didn't find a job in social work, but she was working in a day care center- and she was happy. She thought it was a waste of her degree, but I disagreed. Maybe she would use her degree down the road, but as long as she was happy, and had found her niche in life-as I had- that was all that mattered.

So, I was happy in my professional life. I was respected; with a job I loved, close to home. I was helping others in need. I was making a difference. I thought I would be at the Manor for the rest of my life, or at least until I retired. But like everything else in my life, things didn't always go as planned.

I literally met hundreds of residents and family members during my social work career. Some stood out in my memory more then others. All made their mark in my mind and in my heart.

There was Liz, who lived in the nursing home for thirty years. The wife of a late officer in the army, she was known as the "Mayor of the Manor" because she was around so long. She was a fixture. She delivered the mail each day to her fellow residents. She had the same room, near the window, for years. She was at every activity and party. She often made the local newspaper when they ran a story about the nursing home. And when she died, it affected everyone- fellow residents and staff- very deeply, because she was Phoenixville Manor.

I remember Jim, a really sweet guy who had cancer, but lived in the nursing home for several years. He never complained. He loved the Phillies, and I remember our talks about baseball players back in his day. He told me stories about seeing players like Jimmie Foxx and Babe Ruth- in person.

The modern day player he most admired was an outfielder for the Phillies by the name of Jim Eisenrich. He was a good hitter and a hustler, not an all-star, but a gritty, determined player who never gave up. Jim noticed that, and he called him an "old school player', like those he grew up watching.

On a whim, I decided to write to Jim Eisenrich, with a brief note about our Jim, his situation, and that I thought it would be a great surprise and really make him happy if he could send him an autographed photo to hang in his room. I remembered how great it made me feel, as a kid, when several major league teams sent me autographed souvenirs. I wanted to return the favor.

To my delight, the outfielder sent Jim a personalized photo. I hung it on Jim's wall, and he would stare at that photo with pride. I sent it to his daughter after Jim died. I never told her how Jim got the picture, just that it was his, and he treasured it.

Little things like that, only took a few minutes of time, but made a world of difference to a resident. It was the little extra I tried to do, because I knew how much it meant.

There was Mary, the blind lady whom I visited every day. She had a terrific sense of humor, and we swapped jokes daily to cheer each other up. She asked me how different modern movie stars looked, especially the males, and I kidded about fixing her up with her old crush, Billy Dee Williams.

Actually she fixed me up once. I had several crushes on different nurses and aides at the nursing home over the years, especially a flaming gorgeous redhead named Jill (she was married, but had so much compassion for the residents, and the brightest smile I've ever seen in my life), and a cute blonde named Lisa, who was an aide at the Manor for over ten years, and worked harder then anyone I ever met there. But Mary told her nightly aide, a tall, brunette also named Lisa, that I thought she was cute.

Cute she was! She had to be one of the prettiest girls I ever knew, and I was surprised that she thought I was cute too, and we started dating for a while, thanks to Mary.

I could go on and on about the different residents I met over the years and the impact we had on each other's lives. I couldn't possibly mention all of them, but I would be remiss not to mention one special resident that affected my world while I worked at the Manor and still remains in my thoughts.

His name was Teddy. He was in his early 80s. I very rarely saw Teddy not smiling. His face was impish-like, with a wide grin, pointy ears, and small blue eyes. He refused to have his gray hair cut, which was his right, so he wore it in a ponytail.

Teddy was diagnosed as being mentally retarded, but as I worked with Teddy over the years, and learned more about him and his past, I seriously questioned that diagnosis, and thought he was not diagnosed properly for all those years.

He spent the first thirty-five years of his life in a local mental institution. He did menial jobs such as janitor and cook. I never thought he was truly mentally retarded- maybe "slow"- but not retarded, because he had amazing talents that he developed over the years. He played the harmonica flawlessly, able to play almost any tune by request. He loved Bingo, and even while living in the community, his memory was so precise, he never used Bingo chips to cover his numbers. He memorized the cards.

Things like that made me believe that Teddy, because of a physically disability (he had some sort of muscle disease, maybe Cerebral Palsy, which caused his limbs to be twisted and contorted, and his body to shake violently at times from seizures), he was shut away in a mental institution as an infant. Back in those days when Teddy was growing up, it was not uncommon for someone deemed as "different" to be put away and never heard from again.

Teddy could only learn from what he saw and heard. He was a product of his environment. He never received any formal education. He was more or less used as a slave in the institution, one of the "brighter boys", who helped take care of the needier patients.

During the late 1960s and into the 1970s, Pennsylvania began to assimilate more mental health patients into the community. So Teddy finally left the hospital and lived in a group home with several other gentlemen form the Phoenixville area. He worked in the laundry department of the local hospital for years, earning a paycheck instead of collecting disability. He walked to work every day, through rain and snow, often working twelve-hour days.

He didn't have an easy life. For fun, he loved going to local Bingo games, and attended Bingo almost every night of the week. That was his enjoyment. He never won much, but he was happy. Otherwise, he watched the Phillies.

A few years before I became Social Service Assistant, Teddy had come to the nursing home. A car hit him while he was crossing the street on the way to Bingo. He broke his hip. Already having problems walking, he couldn't rehabilitate well enough to return to the group home, so he ended up staying at the nursing home long term. But it was his dream to eventually walk again, and in the big picture, to move to Florida with his pen pal, a lady he met as a youth at the institution who worked there as a nurse, and who had stayed friends with Teddy over the years. She married and retired to Florida, but still wrote to Teddy, and sent him goodies in the mail often.

Realistic or not, that was Teddy's goal- to walk well enough someday to relocate to Florida and live close to his friend. During the summer, when his friend and her husband traveled north, they would take him out for the day, to the mall, and to a restaurant for Teddy's favorite meal- fried chicken and a chocolate milk shake. He looked forward to that single day each year.

His friend told him, if he could learn to walk, she would consider taking him to Florida. So, it gave Teddy a goal, and he often insisted to the therapists to work with him, even if they thought he could not benefit from any more therapy. Often he would be seen huffing and puffing up and down the hall on the second floor in a special walker, never giving up.

Teddy had family, but they never bothered with him. He had a brother in New Jersey, but Teddy couldn't remember which town he lived in. He also had a brother in the coal mine region of Pennsylvania, but Teddy didn't want anything to do with him. Teddy had tried to visit him a few times in the past, but was always told his brother "wasn't home"", and "not to come back again." Teddy thought his brother was actually hiding form him when he saw him at the door, afraid Ted wanted to "borrow money from him."

He claimed to have one last brother somewhere in Texas, which he did want to find. He thought the last letter he received from that brother came from Killeen, Texas, but he was not sure. After the last letter, Ted broke his hip, ended up in a nursing home, and never heard from that brother again. He probably never knew that Ted was now a nursing home resident. Was he trying to contact Teddy? No letters were ever forwarded to him.

I tried to find the guy over the Internet. I even wrote to the police in Killeen, Texas, explaining the situation and asking for help. They did write back, claiming they looked up old army records, social security numbers, even the local phone book, and no one by that name was ever uncovered.

Teddy may have been confused to the location. He was sharp as a tack in certain areas, but foggy when it came to dates and time, maybe because he had no conception of time, growing up in an institution and having little contact with the outside world.

Still, with or without family, Teddy was happy. He made friends easily with his sense of humor and infectious smile. He claimed to have 'trained" many of the aides working in the nursing home. He knew his routine, how to wash him, how to dress him. Teddy, because he was now wheel chair bound and still suffered from violent tremors at times, could do very little for himself. He was able to hold his harmonica awkwardly in his deformed fingers, use a remote control for his television, but could do very little concerning caring for himself. He even had to be fed, because when he tried to hold a fork or spoon or cup he would more often then not end up spilling the food or drink on himself or the floor.

Still, he didn't complain. He loved watching the Phillies on his little television, staying up late to watch the West Coast games. He had a Phillies pennant and Phillies cap hung on a bulletin board on the side of his bed, along with tons of photos he collected over the years, mostly pictures of former nurses and aides who he had become friends with.

A large picture of Jesus adorned his wall too, and often I would glide by his room and see him sitting quietly during commercials for his soap operas, eyes closed, but praying aloud, quietly, asking God to please help him walk again someday.

A local junior high teacher dressed up as Santa Claus each holiday season, and would visit our residents, passing out cookies, fruit, candy canes and taking Polaroid pictures with the residents. Teddy had a few years' worth of Santa Claus pictures tacked on his bulletin board. He still played Bingo in the nursing home, now excited to win prizes such as bananas rather then big money jackpots. When he didn't win, he still didn't complain, and would mumble to himself, "I'll win next time," as he pushed his chair back to his room. He still never used Bingo chips. When he did win, he let everyone know, hollering at the top of his lungs "Bingo right here," to the disgust of nearby residents. That was his signature call of victory, even in the community. ""Bingo right here!" Everyone in the gaming hall knew it was Teddy who had won.

Teddy was a bit of a flirt too, and he made friends so easily. Often some good-hearted aides would bring him in candy and cookies, and pretty soon his room looked like a grocery store. One aide even took him out to Bingo one night, which pleased him to no end, seeing old friends again. "Everyone thought I was dead," he laughed.

He won $60 that night, and gave the aide half for taking him out.

He loved playing the lottery too, always buying one ticket per week. He played the same numbers. "They gotta come up sooner or later," he would surmise. Why he played those numbers, no one knew, but he never changed them "If they came up, and I didn't play them, I would be sick".

Winning the lottery was part of his plan to move to Florida, hire a private duty nurse to take care of him, and sit out in the sun all day, working on his tan, which he often did in the patio of the nursing home during the summer. Hitting the lottery would just speed up the process someday. He was still determined to see Florida someday, lottery or not.

Teddy was the "Welcome Wagon" of the facility, and he would learn there was a new admission and always wheel through the building and greet a newcomer. He played his harmonica a lot, Christmas carols (even not in season) and Gospel songs were his specialties. Often, he would sit in his room, or out in the hall, and play his harmonica for hours.

He saw many roommates come and go over the years. In total, he spent about thirteen years in the nursing home. He rang the call bell for those roommates who couldn't help themselves yet needed care. He got along with most, although since he was hard of hearing (but refused hearing aides), he would turn up his television loud, sometimes to the annoyance of his roommates.

I grew close to Teddy because I fed him lunch each weekday. He was easy to feed. Every day was the same menu- fried chicken and chocolate ice cream. If chicken weren't available, then it would be macaroni and cheese or a baloney sandwich (hold the mustard).

We talked during lunch. He would tell me about his past, about his dreams of going to Florida someday with his friend, of hitting the lottery, of the Phillies, of how he had won the previous night at Bingo. The conversations rarely varied, but having someone to talk to- especially someone to listen- made Teddy happy.

I could identify with him. Although we were far apart in age, we had some similarities. We both love Baseball. And I looked at Teddy and thought of what could have been in my life. If my parents had not cared so much, they could have easily found a reason to institutionalize me as well when I was a kid. I could relate to Teddy's trial and tribulations in life yet appreciate his simple joys, such as hollering "Bingo!" the chance to declare victory.

Teddy loved to play Checkers. We had a monthly Checker tournament at the nursing home. An older guy named Benny won it almost every month, a former Duke University law student in his early life. A smart guy.

Teddy was no match for Ben, but he tried each month. I volunteered to supervise the matches on Saturdays. I moved the pieces for Teddy, because he was so shaky, he would knock the board over, let alone be able to pick up a checker. He would point to the piece he wanted to move, and to the spot on the board he wished to move to.

I was a pretty good player, from a lot of practice when I was a kid. Ben was good, and had beaten me before, but he wasn't invincible. Teddy could beat him, but he always made one fatal move each match that sealed his fate.

I decided to "help" out my friend a little. Ben was hard of hearing, almost deaf, and he would sit and study the board as we played, rarely looking up. When I saw that Teddy was making an obviously bad move, before I moved the piece I would give out a little cough or negative grunt, a message to say, "Look again". Sometimes he took my advice, sometimes he didn't. When he got fed up with losing for about nine months in a row, steaming back to his room in disgust, he started listening to my noises a little more.

It was funny because sometimes it took Teddy several tries to figure out where he should move. So he would be pointing to one spot on the board, I would let out a hum, then he would quickly point to another square, I would again groan, and he would try another one.

Ben would say, " What the hell are you doing? Come on!" never knowing what was happening, thinking that Teddy was losing it.

I know it was cheating. But I wanted Teddy to win, just once, so badly. Plus Ben would usually gloat after a victory. He knew that he was brighter then Teddy, or most of the seniors he played against. He was the Muhammad Ali of the Checker world.

Well, one Saturday things just fell into place. Teddy played well, and listened to a few suggestions, as Ben seemed to make unusual mistakes. Teddy took the first game of the best-of three match. There was hope, and just the fact that Teddy won one game against Ben was unbelievable.

As I set up the board for the second game I whispered to Ted, "Calm down!" (He was shaking from head to toe). It's only one game. You have to beat him again for the championship. Just play the same way."

Teddy knew most of the usual opening and closing moves. It was the middle game he had problems with. He lost the second game, and it looked like another rout was on.

But to everyone's surprise, Teddy rallied in game three. It was a close match, right down to the end. But when Teddy got ahead a checker, it was just a matter of trading pieces down to the end.

When Teddy finally closed out the victory he let out a yell of joy. Ben went away disgusted, but did smile, saying, "He played good".

We didn't care if it was a tainted victory. It made Teddy happy, and we announced his victory over the intercom system. At least for a month, Teddy was king of the world.

Even after I eventually left the Manor, I tried to stop in to see Teddy every weekend, or when I could. He missed me feeding him lunch each day, but also just missed our talks, and having a friend listen to his stories, even if they were the same stories.

I learned he seemed depressed since I had left, and I called him on the phone to encourage him to eat. He caught Pneumonia that winter. I visited him at the hospital and when he returned to the nursing home.

The last time I saw him he was curled up in bed, moaning. He answered me in whispers, seeming to know I was there, looking at me through tired, glazed eyes, smiling, but so sick; all he wanted to do was sleep.

He died that very week. He never did make it to Florida- but I'm sure he made it to Heaven.

I couldn't attend his funeral. His church had steps. He was buried very decently, as his friend from Florida and local friends chipped in to pay for the expenses.

I did visit his grave later in the day, picking a flower for remembrance.

A few months later I visited his final resting-place again, this time finding a small tombstone. There was an American flag on top, as he used to keep at the side of his wheel chair. But there was also a Bingo card and a Phillies schedule on the stone as well.

Teddy led a tough life, but a life far more important then many people I have met in my life. He was hard to forget. And isn't that all we could ever ask for, not to be forgotten? Teddy made so many friends, and touched so many lives, there was no chance that anyone who was lucky enough to cross his path in life would ever forget him.

It was residents like Teddy who kept me going, Even through tough times, on Mondays when I didn't want to drag myself out of bed in the freezing cold. I knew Teddy was waiting, and I couldn't let him down. He kept the work challenging yet enjoyable, as he appreciated even the simple things in life. He taught me what was truly important- in and out of the nursing home. And every day I left work, and was able to enjoy the sunshine, I felt so lucky.

I never tried to play favorites during my years at the nursing home. But people like Teddy made me believe, every day, that I was doing good work. Fate had chosen me to become a Social Worker, not the other way around. And meeting more residents, like Teddy, in my work, made me just as happy as whatever happiness I may have ever offered in my work.

9. ALL THE TIME

The 1980s were my coming out party. Going to college, finding a girlfriend, becoming more independent. It was a fun time. The 1990s had many highlights too. I was settling in my life, becoming a better social worker, taking more responsibility in my life, and always, learning more.

I became politically involved in my hometown, and advocated for cut curbs on every block of town. Actually it started on my very own street. I was a prisoner on my own block, unable to get off the curb. I wheeled to work every day, since the nursing home was only a block away. But to get across the street, I needed help. I thought this was ridiculous.

I petitioned for the borough to please install cut curbs on my block. They resisted, saying there "was no money". But with the passing of the Americans with Disabilities Act, it was becoming evident that physical barriers needed to be modified, now under law.

As always, attitudes are tough to change. I found the courage to address borough council one night, asking for the curbs, not only for my personal use each day, but also for other disabled and elderly people in our community.

Still, the borough resisted, saying there was no money in the budget to pay for re-construction. I did some research and found that cut curbs were originally planned for my housing development some fifteen or so years earlier, but were never installed. So, they were actually fighting me on something that should have been there in the first place. Maybe it was the builder's fault, but where were the town's inspectors?

When I brought this to light, the council suddenly wanted to help. But before this occurred, a local contractor saw my story in the paper and volunteered his services- material, labor- to fix the curbs on my block, so I could wheel independently to and from work each day.

That was great for me, and I appreciated his help, but now that I was active in this issue, what about the rights of other people in our town?

Soon, cut curbs and ramps began springing up all over town. Phoenixville became more accessible. Maybe it was the new law that finally pushed people to act. But it was just the right thing to do. Now we could see a physical difference, all over town. Maybe this constant reminder was irrating to some, but it opened up a new world to people like myself, and made transportation a lot easier.

I still kept on eye on handicapped parking places in town. Were there enough? What to do with violators? It was so frustrating when all the handicapped spots were taken at the store, and a very able-bodied person emerged from a car in one of those places. I also encouraged local businesses to try and become more accessible too, by adding ramps when possible.

No community will ever be completely accessible, especially in a town like mine, which has many old buildings that cannot be converted or renovated. However it doesn't hurt to try. And if I helped at all with this change, then I was [proud, not only to help myself, but to help others too- especially my own neighbors.

Mom got sick in the early 90s. She was visiting the local pharmacy, became dizzy, and they ended up taking her to the hospital via ambulance. It turned out she had had a heart attack. They thought about doing angioplasty, but her blockage in her heart was so bad- up to 90^ in several arteries- that she needed by-pass surgery.

She had the surgery done at the University of Pennsylvania Hospital, a maze of a place, with outstanding medical personnel. It brought back a lot of memories, back in the city.

I remember waiting there with Mom the morning of the surgery, holding her hand never knowing if I would see her again, trying to keep the mood light with my brothers, yet realizing how serious it was. She was able to talk, and went into the surgery with a lot of faith and hope. I remember all the times she was there for me when I was a kid, offering love and encouragement. Now it was my turn to return the favor.

They ended up doing a quadruple by-pass on her heart- such a strong, caring heart all those years. She spent about a week in the Philadelphia hospital before coming home. She was fighter, and she made it through the surgery. Now she just needed to recover and get her strength back.

Meanwhile, I was doing the best I could at home. My siblings helped me. I ordered out a lot, or went out to eat. I needed to learn how to cook. I had always been sheltered during my life. Now I was responsible for paying bills, making sure the house was running smoothly, all the things people get used to doing and take for granted. Just a natural part of adult life. But to me, every thing was new.

My brother Tom took my shirts to the local dry cleaners each week. I was fairly independent now, so I didn't need much help with my daily care needs. But I couldn't button the top button on my dress shirts, or tie my tie, because of the deformity of my arms, so I needed help. My sister Phyllis would stop over each morning before work and help me. It was a humbling experience, but as I had learned in life, I couldn't be afraid to ask for help if I needed it.

It began to sink in, while Mom was away, not only what she meant to me, and the fact that I needed to appreciate her so much more, but also what my future may be like. If something did happen to her, would I be able to live alone? Take care of myself? Could I handle the house? Or did I need to look into a smaller, place, maybe an apartment?

At times like that, these things go through your mind. Not only was I naturally worried about Mom, although I was encouraged that she would eventually be OK, I worried about my life too. Mom wouldn't be around forever. I had to start thinking about my future, especially since Liv didn't seem to be a part of my life now.

At times I broke down and cried, frustrated when I couldn't do a simple task like buttoning my shirt. Not often in my life did I ever become angry, frustrated, and helpless. But this was really the first time in my life that I was alone. My sister and brothers helped me very much, but they had their lives too. They went home at night, and I locked up, alone. Luckily, my two dogs at the time, Peewee and Fluffy, were good watchdogs and good company.

I got up every day, went to work, return home, change and head to the hospital. After Mom came home, she needed to rest, and she became a bit depressed as well, finding that she couldn't do as much for herself as before. She was always so fiercely independent, and I think this loss of independence, as I saw every day at the nursing home, was a key factor to her moral.

There were brief thoughts of Mom possibly having to admit to the nursing home for a while to get stronger. I could imagine how hard it would be, to not only have a family member in a nursing home, but to be a social worker in that very home. What if it turned out to be long-term? We would deal with it, as my families had. It gave me a new appreciation for the families, and what they went through.

My own Uncle Henry and Aunt Sue both eventually ended up in the nursing home where I worked. That was hard, remembering them as they were in the past, then seeing them fade away into Dementia, depression and physical decline. I would try to see them each day, and felt so helpless when they either asked to go home, or needed something I could not give them. I felt close to my residents anyway, but to have loved ones there, it killed me, especially when I knew they were not going to get any better.

Mom did come home and got well. She was back at her Bingo in a few months, driving again, the doctors giving her at least another good ten years added to her life. I hated to see it happen, especially for Mom, and how close she had come to death, but in another way, it changed all of our lives. It brought our family closer together. It made us all appreciate Mom more, realizing before it's too late, that life is too short, and be gone without warning.

Her illness made me become more independent too, which ultimately molded me into not only a better social worker, but a better person too.

Speaking of which, we threw Mom a surprise party for her 80th birthday. . She never had a party before in her life, and she deserved one. Tracy (Mark's wife), Phyllis and me planned the party for several months. We rented a local hall, had a caterer make the food, sent the invitations, and bought the decorations. It was a lot of work but fun. But maybe the hardest part was keeping it a secret from Mom.

She was a crafty one, and knew something was up the closer we got to April 11th. We invited close family members, friends, and especially her beloved Bingo buddies.

She was very surprised on that Sunday afternoon, as my sister had to think of an excuse to get her to the hall. She was a little embarrassed and kind of mad at first, not really wanting the attention. But afterwards she admitted it was nice.

I always thought one should appreciate someone you love while you can. Don't wait until it's too late. I wish I 'd told my Dad how I felt about him while he was still alive. But I was young, and his illness hit us so suddenly. I was determined not to let that happen with Mom. I hoped she would be around a long time. And a signature birthday party isn't a sign of closing a book- I felt it should be a celebration of life, not the end. It was a great time to look back, but also appreciate her life.

We remembered how special she was to every one. How she would always send out get-well cards, visited people in hospitals, her strong faith in God. The more we thought about it, the more we realized she truly was a special person.

I may have appreciated her more then anyone, just knowing the sacrifice she and Dad made for me when I was a kid. Even now, she continued to care and think about me, worried, even when she was being wheeled into surgery for her by-pass surgery. She worried if I had lunch yet. That was Mom, always thinking of others.

Her party was also important for those who attended. It gave them a chance to express their love, not just through gifts, but also by the honor of the presence.

My brother Jim videotaped part of the party. It would always be a remembrance, not only of the occasion, but also of Mom herself.

It proved to be interesting for years to come, because as time went by, several of the guests, especially some of Mom's older friends had passed away. She would watch the tape and recall fondly how good it was to see her family and friends at such a happy occasion.

I knew it had to be tough on Mom, seeing many of her friends die. I imagined we all would go through that, if we lived long enough, and it reminded me of my residents at the nursing home and how they must feel when they learn a roommate, a friend, a fellow resident, had gone before them.

I was so happy we decided to throw Mom the party. She had always been good to me. Now it was my turn to be good to her. It was a hallmark moment in all of our lives. For Mom, it was a day to remember; a day to truly realize how many people in her life cared about her. But for every one else, it was a moment to cherish forever, a good feeling inside that we had not only made her happy, but we had created a special memory for every one as well.

During the 90s I bought the house from Mom. Not that Mom was going anywhere, but we all thought it was a good idea. Mom always worried about what might happen to me when she passed on. Now, she felt better, knowing I would have a place to live. I thought about the future. I thought about maybe getting a small apartment, which I could easily take care of.

But mom didn't like that idea. She didn't want to leave her home, especially since we now had a pet dog named Louie (he had a nice backyard to run in). So we remodeled the house one spring- new carpets, new paint job. We bought a small stackable washer and dryer and put it upstairs so Mom wouldn't have to climb the basement stairs. We tried to make life easier for both of us.

When Mom courageously bought our rancher after Dad died, over twenty years before, her goal was to make life easier for me. Now it was my turn to return the favor.

Now it was my responsibility to pay the bills. Mom helped me, as we helped each other. But it kept me motivated, knowing I now had a house to maintain.

I thought about how far I had come: from a very dependent disabled individual to a more independent young man- with a credit card! Again, life was new to me, this world of credit cards, cell phones and computers. I began to see how the other half lives, still very modestly on my social worker's wages, but how it felt to have responsibility in life.

I found that more people respected me. They talked to me, not at me. They took me more seriously. I had made something of myself in life, and I felt so proud. I had always thought of myself as not being disabled, maybe to a fault, especially in the romance department. I did have to admit, at least physically, I was different then most. But in my mind and soul I didn't feel any different. I always thought that society labeled me as different. It was a label I would never cease to try and overcome.

Owning the house made me believe even more that I really wasn't different. Sure, it still felt strange to go through most of my life as a very dependent person, and now here I was, a brand new world ahead of me. Some times I wished for those carefree days when I didn't have to worry about things like the electric bill. But deep down inside, I knew that I never wanted to go back to those days. I had come too far to ever give up again.

Who knows what would happen down the road? Would I find a girl? Would I sell the house in time, unable to care for it? All of that was in the future, but for more, I had something to call my own.

I thanked Dad every day because it was really his house. He worked for so many years at the tire plant. And if he didn't die, if Mom had not gotten the money from his retirement to buy the new house, I may have never achieved all I did in life. Moving into the rancher was a huge step towards my independence and growth. And even though dad never lived to see the house, it still was his house- and always would be.

My O.I. was pretty much under control in the 90s. Oh, I would still suffer stress fractures from time to time, and always have a good amount of Arthritis, which I would really feel when the weather changed. But no more fractures, thank God. I was able to lead a relatively "normal" life.

Probably my worst medical ailment was my kidney stones. Kidney stones- I never knew I had them, until one Sunday afternoon in May. It was the day before Memorial Day, and suddenly I became violently ill, with a sharp, knifing pain in my back. I couldn't move, and began breaking out in a cold sweat. Worst of all I had blood in my urine.

Mom missed 11:00 mass for once in her life. After all her prayers and saintly deeds, the good Lord had to forgive her for missing this particular Sunday, thanks to me.

I was scared because I had never felt that way before and didn't know what was going on. I tried to lie down but the pain was unbearable. So we called 911 and they rushed me to the hospital.

As we waited, Mom held my hand. I told her that I loved her, wishing I had done so more often. Why is it that we only take time to express love during very happy or very sad times?

I also thought of Liv, wondering if I would ever see her again.

It is a funny feeling, hearing the distance siren growing closer with each passing moment, knowing they were coming for me. But I was used to ambulances. Often I would hear sirens wailing in the night, piercing the silence, and wondering whom the poor soul was they were intended for.

I knew one of the paramedics from my work at the hospital. And nursing home. I wasn't up to reminiscing, just too scared and feeling too lousy to think anymore. I just wanted to get to the hospital and have them stop whatever was going on in my body.

It was a beautiful, warm, sunny day, with puffy white clouds floating overhead as they took me on the stretcher outside, the ambulance parked in our driveway.

I saw more familiar faces in the emergency room. By now I was feeling a little better, like when you are in the dentist office and all of a sudden your toothache, is gone.

After numerous testing and more needles, which I should have been used to by then, they found I was the proud owner of five kidney stones, all located in my left kidney. One little bugger, probably tired of renting my body, was trying to ease its way down to my bladder, hence the pain and illness.

Kidney stone? I never had any problems with my kidneys. In fact, I had always been proud of my kidneys, as were others. My Uncle Henry had often shook his head in amazement down the casino when he asked if I needed to use the men's room, and I declined. "I can't get over it," he would say. "What do you got, a hose down there?"

I laughed about it then, lying on the hard table, waiting for more test results.

The plan was to go home, strain my urine for a couple of days, and watch if a stone passed. If so, fine. If not, then more tests would be done.

I was between a rock and a hard place, so to speak. In one way, I wished there were a stone to pass so I could forego those tests. On the other hand, passing this stone would be the pits. I heard stories about kidney stones, always with a pained look on the face of the teller. I kept envisioning boulders in my dreams.

Three days passed, but that was all that passed. So I returned to the hospital for the IVP test. I wasn't allowed to eat any solid food the day before the test. I soon grew tired of juice, Jello and soup. I couldn't wait to eat a hoagie, wondering if a liquid diet would be my fate forever.

Fear of the unknown was the biggest worry. Sitting in the waiting room I was beginning to get cold feet, but by now it was too late to back out.

After my initial attack I was feeling better. Did I pass the stone without even knowing it? If I still had stones, could they be treated with medication, ultra-sound therapy, and avoid surgery? Or was it something other then stones?

They shot some kind of dye into my arm before taking a series of abdominal x-rays. I had to sign a consent form before the injection was given. There was a slight chance that the dye could prove to be fatal. An allergic reaction was possible.

It wasn't much of a choice between kidney stones and a lethal dose of dye. With all the x-rays I had in my time, I should have been glowing by then, so a few more wouldn't matter.

When they finally confirmed I had the stones, my family doctor referred me to a specialist, a urologist who looked nearly as young as I was.

"You'll be seeing a lot of me in the years to come," he said.

Actually, the doc had some good news. True, I was the owner of stones, but they were located in a part of my left kidney where they weren't blocking anything, other then the one causing the pain, which was still slowly working its way down to my bladder and other important areas.

He decided I could pass this guy, and watch my progress over time. No surgery for now. But I did need to start drinking water- a lot of water- between eight to ten glasses a day. Drinking an ocean would be better then getting cut.

Eventually I was able to pass this tenant, as I did with the rest, except for one. This stone was larger then the rest, and my urologist, Dr. Rose, felt no way would I be able to pass it. So I was in the hospital as an outpatient, and he lasered the stone, without having to cut me, like he was playing a video game.

With the passing of each stone, there was a time of pain, of waiting. It depended how quickly or slowly these jagged little guys wanted to move. Some I was able to pass at home, with medicine to help ease the pain. Some, they wanted to keep an eye on the progress in the hospital. Usually I was in for a few days, as the nurses pushed fluids and hooked me up to Ivs.

The nurses used to kid me, that having a stone was just like having a baby-very painful. I didn't know about the baby thing. But I did know about the pain. Even through my broken bone years, some of this kidney stone pain was at times much more intense.

After passing a stone, my entire body let out a deep sigh. It was amazing how such a small article could make an entire body feel so miserable.

Unlike having a baby, I couldn't even keep my stone, not that I would want to. I named each one: "Rocky", Mick Jagger" (Rolling Stone?). But after passing a stone, the nurses would whisk it away in a test tube and send it down to the lab for analysis. I never even had a chance to say goodbye.

In the years to come I would have to watch my diet, drink a lot of water, and go for annual check-ups. Otherwise, there wasn't much to do. Having a stone was always like having a sword hanging over your head. You just never knew when it might decide to move and want out. I didn't let it control my life, but I couldn't forget about them. Some were too small to laser, but they were allow to sit and rest, or grow large enough to laser before they did any damage." Let sleeping stones lie" was our motto.

One of the proudest moments of the 90s was when my youngest brother Mark, and his fiancée, Tracy, asked me to be Best Man at their wedding. This meant a lot to me, because I was beginning to think I might never get married. I had always hated weddings, like funerals. There was dancing at weddings, and I couldn't dance. I just always felt so out of place. I knew it was my fault feeling that way. But weddings were actually sort of depressing to me, knowing that deep down inside, I loved them, but always wanted it to be me, but knowing that it probably never would be me.

Anyway, when my brother asked me to be his Best Man, I accepted immediately. He knew I couldn't do some of the usual Best Man traditions, like throwing a bachelor party the night before the wedding. But I was happy he knew it meant so much to me, that he didn't care about the other things that went with the honor.

It was the first time-and maybe the last- I would wear a tuxedo, and I actually looked pretty good. It was all kind of exciting, all the preparations, getting fitted for the tux, the rehearsal. Maybe the most nervous part of the whole thing was trying to think of a witty, sincere toast for the reception. It was the Best Man's job to make a champagne toast, and I thought about what to say for weeks, changing my mind several times. Should I try to be funny? What to say?

On the wedding day, I was sitting up front with Mark standing beside me, and I knew he was understandably nervous, so I tried to keep the moment light, get him relaxed, loosen up, quipping, "I told the limo driver to keep the car running. It's not too late to run," I joked.

Hey-it was only the most important day in the guy's life-why be so serious about it?

I think I did all right, even finding the wedding ring, and Mark and Tracy thanked me after, like I had done something special. It was they who had done something special, not me.

The site of the reception was in a very historic building near town. There were steps to get to the actual reception hall, flights of steps. Guys offered to pull my chair up the steps. I always held my breath going up or down, the fear of falling still with me from my childhood. Not that I didn't trust these guys. But I worried more about getting back down, after the reception, especially since some of these big guys might be a little woozy.

But then Tracy's cousin came to my rescue. He was then a star football player for Penn State University, Brad Scioli, Defensive End. He went about 6'5, maybe 280 pounds. Big guy! He later would go on to play professionally for the Indianapolis Colts.

He was at the wedding. After meeting Brad, I felt a lot better. He learned that I needed help getting up the three flights of stairs- and he literally picked up my chair-with me in it- and carried it up the steps. No problem. He did the same thing on the way back. To him I must have felt like a sack of potatoes.

At the reception we had wine at the table. Now, I never was a big drinker. But I enjoyed a glass of wine with an Italian meal (my favorite). But then I had the champagne with my toast. The toast went well, and I went blank anyway with any formulated speeches, just as I did in Math class and when I met Barry Manilow. The mind went totally blank.

So, I just kept it simple and short- and sincere. I wished them the best of luck, and let them know what an honor it was for me, to be involved.

Well, after the wine and champagne, I was feeling no pain. But then Mark came over, a little blitzed himself, and insisted that it was a tradition for the groom and best man to do a vodka shot, straight up.

Yowsa! It was only a small shot, but I never felt so looped and happy in my life. The room was spinning, and if I could've been sited for drunk driving, I was guilty. Toes were almost crushed everywhere I wheeled. I felt like doing wheelies, my hands suddenly unable to steer or even push the damn chair. Push? How do you push?

I didn't get sick, nor have a hangover. But it did take me a while to remember that I couldn't walk.

All in all, it was a memorable time. I hoped that someday, I could return the favor. But even if it never happened, I would never forget that wedding.

The computer entered my life again in the 90s. I finally got a home PC and loved it. I used it for work, doing research, writing, but I also used it for fun too. One of the ways I used the computer was to meet new friends.

The computer became the CB radio of the modern age. It allowed me to reach out and make friends with others, especially with people who had common interests. I placed ads in the personals, and answered ads. I made local friends, but also made friends in different states and international countries.

Emailing was easy. If I still wanting to write something personal, there was nothing like pen and paper, as when Liv and I were pen pals. But emailing was fun and let me reach friends quickly.

I made some really good friends over the Internet, which had a bad reputation for dating. Some of my off-line friends, such as Vicki, had computers now, and we would keep in touch on the net. At first I didn't mention my disability in my personal profile. That was a mistake, in my opinion. I would get to know someone, then have to explain about my wheel chair. Many women claimed to not care, and I guess it really didn't matter to someone who lived in Idaho who I may never meet anyway.

But to local friends, people I did hope to meet someday, it did matter. It wasn't fair, to get to know someone, then drop a bombshell, and hope they understood, or worse, don't say anything until we met. Are you the same Greg I email and talk to each day?

So I decided to include the wheel chair in my profile. That way, people could either get to know me from the start, and accept me as I was, or move on. It saved a lot of hurt feelings. Most of all, it was honest.

People tended to come and go on the computer, as they had on the CB radio. Again, for me, it was hard finding a way to meet people. I wasn't a bar person, and driving once again was a major barrier in my life. I know that I came off as a total loser, and couldn't use my disability as an excuse. I couldn't blame if a girl didn't answer my ad or didn't want to get involved. Who wanted the hassle of having to deal with the chair?

Sure, I had my advantages too. But most of the time I was rejected, even for friendship. I was again learning that although physical barriers were coming down in society, prejudices were much more difficult to overcome.

What was I looking for? Always more friends. A special companion, someone to share dinner and a movie with, and someone who just cared about how my day went. Someone to look forward to talking to, emailing and getting letters, a friend to share feelings and ideas with.

Was I looking for another Liv? Yes, I admit it would've been nice to find someone special, someone with common interests, and someone who would be my soul mate in time. But there was only one Liv. And although I couldn't hide in a cave, and needed to each out, I couldn't expect magic to happen again.

On the contrary, more bad things happened. I'll never forget one girl I had met on line. She seemed very nice, and we emailed each other for weeks. She didn't live too far away, and eventually we started talking on the phone.

She knew about my disability, and claimed it "didn't matter". I had heard that line before, but with each time, I hoped it was for real.

We planned to meet. It was a good idea to meet in a neutral location, a public place such as a restaurant, but in my situation, it was hard getting to places. So she agreed to meet me in front of my house.

She did show up, and she was friendly, but I learned about people over the years, and although she claimed everything was fine, I knew from her sudden quietness and the fact she didn't look in my eyes that my disability effected her.

I guess it all sunk in. Gee, he really is in a wheel chair! What did I get myself into?

Well, the plan was to talk, watch a video and just have a nice night, just like the nights we had spent weeks before, talking on line or on the phone. But after a few minutes she said she needed to go to her car and "recharge the battery in her car phone", and would be right back. I said fine, and waited for her inside.

I waited and waited and waited. After about ten minutes or so, I looked outside. I wheeled down the ramp to the driveway. Her car was gone. She had taken off, without even saying goodbye. I felt so devastated.

I guess she just couldn't handle it. Many people, myself included, got too wrapped up in fantasy on the net- wishing and hoping to find a perfect someone. In reality, most people turned out to be not so perfect, and that is where the letdown came in.

I let her down, because I wasn't what she expected me to be like. She let me down too, because she just took off. I cried that night, but in time, I went on with life. I couldn't condone what she had done, but I could understand the feelings of anxiety and uneasiness.

Usually after a date, I would at least get a letter in my mailbox the next day, something to the tone of "You're a great guy but..." At first I was bitter and angry, and either would vent in return out of frustration or not answer at all. Even so-called able-bodied people don't always click, and I had to learn the rules of the dating game, which were different on line. I was rejected and hurt, but if I wanted to make friends and maybe meet someone special, I had to accept the good with the bad. Either that or stay off line.

I learned to find more people on line that shared my common interests. I even sought out a disability board, and made friends there. I still wasn't buying into the idea of "because you are disabled, you should only date other disabled people". But at least I was finding friends who may understand, friends who may share feelings and know what it was like to feel different, and feel happiness too. Their stories and encouragement gave me hope.

In many ways I had grown in my life- my job, my house- but in other ways, I seemed frozen in time, like in relationships. I wasn't getting any younger. Suddenly, women in their 20s and 30s were too young for me. I was growing old-alone.

I never forgot Liv. In time the anger and bitterness went away. I missed her. So I started returning her occasional cards. For the next several years we were friends, coming full-cycle, back to pen pals again. She could have told me to take the hint, move on in life, but she didn't. She wanted to remain friends too. And that gave me hope that we could start fresh again.

The bitterness had vanished. It was good to see mail from her again. When she got a computer we would email. But there was nothing like the old way of communicating, by paper and pen. We wrote about family, work and always Manilow. She told me about the new condo she had bought in Oslo, and how she wanted me to visit someday.

It was good to have her in my life again.

To my surprise, Liv wrote me around 1996 and told me she was coming to America to attend a convention in Las Vegas. She wondered if she could possibly visit the Grand Canyon- and me- in the same trip?

At first I was scared by this idea. Oh, how I wanted to see her again! But this would be the first time since the break-up, and although the anger was far in the past, I still felt awkward about meeting her again.

Then I thought, hey, grow up! She was special to you. You always loved when she visited. Life is too short Face your fears head-on, stay positive and see what happens.

By now, Liv knew the routine. She would take the airport van to King of Prussia, where we would pick her up. As we waited for the van to appear, those old butterflies soared in my stomach again, just like the first time we met, ten years earlier. Funny, we had grown so at ease with each other over the years, yet now, it was like meeting a stranger once more.

When she stepped off the van, we hugged. No kiss but better then a handshake. We both felt a little uncomfortable at first, remembering the past, but it was so good to see her. We were together, through thick and thin, no matter what.

For that week we were strictly pals, which was a good foundation to build on. I didn't expect her to rush into my arms and romance would suddenly reappear like before- although I had hopes.

We went to the mall, the movies, and our favorite restaurants again. We intended to talk about the break-up, but each time we tried, words would not surface, and we would quickly change the subject, avoiding the subject. Deep down inside we both knew that sooner or later it would come up.

The closest we came to discussing the matter was a night in our favorite Italian restaurant, chatting over a glass of red wine. Liv suddenly looked across the table at me, after we laughed about some fond memory. Laughing, her eyes glazed at mine, transfixed for such a long time. She softly said, "I'm sorry."

I wondered how it would come up. With tears? In anger? Or not at all?

My eyes clouded with tears, the sentimental fool I was. All the years of frustration, yet loving her- and here we were- together. No ocean between us, no letters to separate us. I bit my lower lip and simply. whispered, " It's OK," taking her hand.

That is all we said. I think that is all we ever needed to say. We both felt a sense of relief, more relaxed, all the years of guilt and sorrow wiped away. We could begin to heal and feel again.

On our way home from the movies one night, a car pulled up beside us. Were they looking for directions? It was a woman in the car, and she rolled down her window.

"Sorry, I just have to ask, " she said shyly. "Were you two on TV a while ago?"

We said yes, surprised that someone had remembered. our brush with fame so long ago. The woman wished us luck before driving off, and we looked at each other and just smiled.

Maybe that vacation was for closure. Maybe we would continue our friendship, maybe a relationship down the road. But for now, we needed closure. One needs to close a door before opening another.

The next time we met was in 1999, as we continued to write in between. Barry was on tour that year and he was scheduled to play the new outdoor venue in Camden, New Jersey, just across the river from Philly.

This time, I asked if she wanted to come over for the show. She answered yes.

We went to the concert with Vicki and Chris. It was like old times again. Seeing Barry perform together was always special. That night was also memorable for another reason. That entire summer was so hot and humid, with little rain. A drought for months. Every thing was brown and dry, thirsting for water.

Well, on the night of the concert Philadelphia received a tremendous thunderstorm, the likes I had never seen before. From our seats, about halfway up the venue, we could see the river and the city skyline. The flashes of lightning looked like sparkling fireworks in the sky, growing more intense as the storm approached.

Then the cool rains came, in sheets. Luckily we were under the roof. Those poor people on the lawn got drenched and scattered for shelter, some running to the parking lot, while others attempted to cram under the roof for protection.

The torrents of wind-blown rain flooded the aisles. Ushers used giant brooms to sweep the growing puddles into the drains. It was so surreal, hearing the "whoosh" of the brooms whisking the water away, as Barry sat on the edge of the stage singing- of all songs- a beautiful acoustic rendition of "Somewhere Down The Road"- our song.

With the fierce lightning flashing nearby we really thought they might end the show early, even though it had just begun. We wouldn't have minded, for Barry and the band members' safety that's how bad it was.

But the show went on. No encores, which wasn't a surprise. After an evening of braving electrocution, I couldn't blame him for wanting to get out of there and head for the next gig.

Liv turned to me and laughed. Out of all the concerts and times together, this was one of the strangest, yet most memorable evenings. It proved that surprises could still happen.

We raced to the car after the show, and although we had a handicapped spot, we got soaked anyway. That was all right. It added to the fun, and gave us a taste of what the lawn people went through.

In the car, dripping wet, I kidded Liv, "You must be our good luck charm. All the way from Norway, and it rains."

We could have used an ark that night to get home, but we made it.

The morning she left for home I went into her room and said goodbye. Like the old days, I hated to say bye. I had to work that day, so I was dressed in a shirt and tie so early in the morning. Mom would take Liv to meet the van at noon.

I was still afraid to touch her, but wanted to so much. Tears again began to well in my eyes, but this time Liv made it easier. She reached out and hugged me, whispering in my ear "You have been so great."

"I still love you," I admitted.

"I know you do," she replied. "Don't worry. I'll be back."

She did come back. Liv would always be special to me. Life goes on, but she would always be in my heart. Who knew what the future would hold? Maybe after her student loans were paid off, maybe she would think again about us? Or maybe we would always just be friends. I learned over the years that a good friend like Liv was hard to find. Maybe I would never find another love like we had. But I did know one thing-I never wanted her out of my life again.

We were back in Atlantic City during a future visit, the memories warming us, as we looked at the ocean from the boardwalk, watching the purple sunset. I gingerly asked if she had a boyfriend, if she had found someone new. Never asked her before. I was afraid of the answer, but needed to know.

"No," she answered calmly. "And I'm not looking either." She gently touched the back of my neck, letting me know everything would be fine.

I wished our relationship had ended with marriage, kids, living happily ever after. But as of now, we remain friends.

Over the years I had become a fan of singer/songwriter Richard Marx, and even met him a few times. He is really a nice guy. Bobby Rydell will always be special in my life. But I can never forget how Barry Manilow and his music changed my life.

Barry Manilow still remains important in our lives, and we catch him when we can, together, when we are on the same continent. Liv occasionally flies to London to see him there, I see him locally (like during a Christmas concert at a casino, when he had the audience singing carols- at 1:00 in the morning). We buy every new CD (including the box set- over 70 songs of Manilow rarities. As Barry said, "You'll either love it, or it will drive you up the damn wall!"). The older CDs remain special too, as they contain so many memories.

I'm glad he has made a "comeback" recently, especially after the success of "Ultimate Manilow", a greatest hits collection. But to the fans, he never really went away. He has been in our lives always, and his music would remain with us forever.

His posters still hang in my room. Old ticket stubs and photographs are treasured in scrapbooks. There is even a life-sized beach towel of Barry hanging on the inside of my bathroom door. Is that scary or what?

Most of all, whenever I still hear a Manilow song, my heart skips a beat. I think of Liv. Not only of the past, but the future too. I smile, happiness in my heart, knowing that "somewhere down the road" magic could happen again- only this time, lasting forever.

I never thought it would happen Things were changing at the nursing home. We had gotten a bad state inspection in 1998, luckily not effecting my department, but still, we were in it as a team, so everyone felt the aftermath.

Other then clearing up the deficiencies, our Administrator, Mrs. Alfgren, was asked to step down. It was sad, because it was forced, and after nearly twenty years at the nursing home, we all imagined she would retire gracefully, on her own terms. But the corporation was not so sentimental, and she was asked to leave.

I remember her last day. She had become administrator around the same time that I had started as a volunteer. She sat in my office and stared at me, mumbling, "Well, Greg, we have been through a lot together,"

I hoped they would give her another chance, but she admitted that maybe it was time to step down. She was in her 70s. She could still work, part-time, maybe volunteer, and finally enjoy her free time. But I knew it had to be so hard for her, because that facility and those residents were her life for so many years, especially after her husband had died. Her work was her life. Now she was forced to give it up.

After she left, things changed. A new Administrator took over, and much of the staff left either on their own or not. She wanted her own people on board, so if they didn't resign voluntarily, she was determined to make the job tough enough to consider leaving.

I always thought I would retire from that nursing home. It was my dream job, where it all began, so close to home, plus I loved the work.

But as the other staff I had worked with for so long began to quit, I felt more and more alone. Assistants came and went, and the new administrator took her time in finding replacements. I ended up doing three jobs in one- admissions, the assistant's position and my own. I repeatedly asked for help, and they even took the ad out of the paper, thinking that since I was doing the work, why look?

I began to burn out, feeling both physically and mentally exhausted. The final straw came with my annual evaluation. I always felt I had done a good job. Sure, I was always learning, which was good, but I never had very many complaints form residents or families.

One weekend nursing admitted an elderly couple from the community, in an effort to fill beds, a couple who were more suited to assisted living rather then nursing home care. Medicaid refused to pay for their stay, and the administrator then asked them to leave. They weren't getting paid, and everyday spent in the nursing home meant money being lost by the corporation.

I was asked to find them a place to go-quickly. I tried, but no other nursing home wanted to take the chance we had. They had no friends or family to take them. I searched beyond the area for an affordable facility where they could live, plus as equally important, a place they wanted to go.

I finally contacted a local friend who agreed that the couple could live with his family. By then, even though I had successfully found them a home, I was blamed for not finding them a place to go fast enough.

Again, money talked, and this was reflected in my evaluation. Our nursing "home" was feeling more like a nursing "business".

Residents were being moved to other rooms, without their consent or without their family or new roommate being informed. This was against Residents' Rights. So was abuse, both verbal and physically, both of which I suspected of going on at times. When I reported my concerts to the new Administrator and Director of Nursing, my concerns were being brushed off.

I always felt I was an advocate for the residents. Even though I was being paid by the facility, my moral allegiance was still to my residents, and I protested, again on deaf ears.

I guess they never thought I would quit. I had been a fixture at the nursing home for so long. It was a good job, I still liked working with the residents and it was convenient. And if I did look for another job, would I find one, let alone a position so close to home?

I felt trapped, and didn't know what to do. Things weren't getting any better. I resisted resigning because I knew that is exactly what the administrator wanted. I hung in there as long as I could, especially for the residents, until one overwhelming day, I decided I just couldn't take it anymore.

So I gave my two weeks' notice. I began to realize what Mrs. Alfgren had gone through only months earlier.

Mom supported my decision, but again my family and friends didn't really understand. Here I was, walking away again, from a job; especially from one I wanted so long. I wasn't even sure, in my heart, that I was doing the right thing. But that little voice inside, one I learned to listen to during my life, one that was rarely wrong, told me to do it, that everything would be fine.

I couldn't see how. I didn't have another job lined up. I dreaded the thought of sending out resumes again; of perhaps trying to collect unemployment or disability once more, of starting over, when I should have been settling into my career.

Those final two weeks were so difficult. The residents couldn't believe I was leaving. I visited each one, spending time to talk. The staff was sad to see me go too, especially the veterans, but near the end I was getting the cold shoulder routine, like I was now an outsider, that I was the quitter. They knew there were problems with Administration, but I got the feeling I was letting everyone down.

And maybe I was- including myself.

On my last day, some of the veterans threw me a "retirement" party- that's how the Administrator justified my leaving to the angry residents and families- that I had chosen to "retire"- even though I had barely turned 40.

My disability was getting worse. It wasn't allowing me to do my job as I once had. I needed time to rest, to take it easy. I couldn't cut it anymore according to the administrator.

After the party I slowly wheeled down the hall for the last time to my office. I remembered all the faces, the people I had met, and the needy I had helped over the years. People like John and Teddy. I cleaned out my desk and headed home.

Even though I was no longer a social worker at the nursing home, nothing could stop me from visiting my residents. At first I tried to stay away, trying to allow some distance to grow. But I could never forget people like Teddy, or even my own Aunt Sue, who was then a resident as well. I would often visit on Sunday, partly to avoid bumping into the Administrator, and partly because during the week I was busy looking for another job.

As fate would have it, the Montgomery County Geriatric Center, the facility I had applied to in the past, had kept my resume on file. When the Director of Social Services, Diane, was involved in a car accident, and needed to recuperate for several months, they suddenly needed an experienced social worker.

The Assistant Administrator called me, asked me to interview, and in only a day, offered me a position. It would be in the Pre-Admissions Department. I quickly accepted.

I was happy to work again. The Geriatric Center was only ten minutes from home. I arranged for the paratransit to take me to and from work each day.

I quickly learned my new job, meeting families prior to admission, gathering information, completing social histories, and conducting tours. It was different then what I had done before, and I missed working with residents directly, but I liked the new challenge, the new goals, and the Center treated its employees very well. Most of all, I was happy.

When Diane returned to work I stayed. As of now, I still work at the Center, providing emotional support to residents and families, especially prior to an admission. I see much guilt, grief, anger and depression regarding placement. But I feel I'm an important part of the team, often the very first person people meet or talk to when they inquire about placement. I use the many contacts I had made over the years, and once word got around that I had changed jobs, even some residents from my former nursing home transferred over.

Finally, one of my proudest moments in the 90s occurred in spring of 1999. I met Rick while I was still working at the Manor several years earlier. He was a social worker from a private agency that was contracted to help us on a weekly basis. Rick was an excellent, caring social worker, soft-spoken, thoughtful, and a middle-aged, handsome guy. He worked as a counselor for this particular agency, but also did private practice too. He helped us out by not only counseling individually, especially with those more difficult residents who had mood or behavior problems, but also group work too.

The residents loved him, especially the ladies, and once in a group, they looked forward to attending each week, and many didn't want to leave the group once their goals were achieved.

He eventually left the agency and started teaching at West Chester University, my old school. We kept in touch over the years, and he always encouraged me to visit the campus again, and especially wanted me to stop by and talk to his senior practicum class each semester.

Every time he asked, I thought of an excuse not to go. But in spring of 19999 Rick called me, and asked me to reconsider. He was going to a seminar in England for a week, and needed someone to fill in for his practicum class. He thought I would be a good example for his students, of a guy who made it in social work, overcoming a few obstacles on the way.

I think he knew it might do me good too, returning to the campus, meeting his students. Plus it would help him out too.

I finally agreed, taking a day off from work, and scheduling paratransit. The class would go from 1 to 4. I wrote up a tentative agenda, talking about my past, which Rick insisted on, listening to the students' questions and thoughts about their internships, and finally, offering a few tips about life out of school in the field.

I liked the idea. I thought it would have been cool for an experienced social worker to stop into my old class and let me know what to expect, and maybe how to avoid mistakes. It is true- everyone needs to learn on their own, and there are certain things one can't be taught in a classroom. Plus it was a way of giving something back to Rick and to West Chester.

I dressed in a suit and tie and arrived at the classroom before one o'clock, waiting for the students to arrive. I wasn't sure what, if anything, Rick had told them about me. As they filed in, they said hello, cautiously, surprised at my appearance.

I was a little nervous, but felt better about public speaking over the years, after doing seminars at work, family council meetings and that communications class I took way back at West Chester.

My plan was to try not to be too boring or talk too much. I wanted to learn about the students, and try to help solve any problems, and other then tell them about my past, try to maintain Rick's objective for the weekly class. We formed a circle and just talked.

The students were pretty quiet as they listened to my story, although I encouraged questions. As I spoke I could see myself in those seats just a mere ten years earlier. The memories flooded back-not only of my social work courses but of all my years in school, and especially of my years of turning my life around. I even thought about my childhood, my days battling O.I. and all the days spent in hospitals.

The final hour of the class was my favorite. I know the students wanted out by then, even though we took several breaks during the afternoon, so I tried to keep it light.

I basically spoke from the heart, with a few notes, and tried to answer questions and anticipate questions a student may be curious to know.

A few items would come to mind: Go for your Masters? It depends. If you can afford it, go for it. Once out of school, it's hard to go back. Getting back into the routine of studying is tough. A Masters allows one more flexibility in the field, make more money and hopefully help more people. But I always was a hands-on social worker, not one to sit behind a desk and give orders. Many positions in the field require a Masters, so continuing on with education was almost necessary. But if one couldn't afford to stay in school, or just wanted to get out there and start working, or didn't have the time for both work and school, then a Bachelor's Degree is nothing to sneeze at.

Writing and paperwork would always be part of the job, no matter what the social work position. Can't get away from it. Spending time with the clients was most important and hopefully makes up for time spent completing forms.

I learned one didn't have to travel into the city to find a decent job. But, as in my case, sometimes one has to be in the right place at the right time. Be persistent. Have a goal and never give up trying to obtain that goal.

I learned to make contacts in the field, and advised the students to use each other, even after graduation, for support and guidance, or as job sources. Only another social worker really knows what one is going through. I warned about stress, not getting burned out, taking time to enjoy life. Important not to take your work home with you, to learn to separate your professional life from your personal life. Stress management was key. Tomorrow is another day. You do the best you can each day, but when you leave work, you leave everything at work.

Common sense was a big part of social work. Theories and whatever one learns in school were important, but social work really came down to feelings and common sense. Sure, using tips and techniques taught in school were important, but in a fast-paced atmosphere, you don't always have time to think. You have to react, and go from experience and instinct. Much of that comes with time.

Finally, I thought that feelings were important. Never underestimate using empathy, listening to others. Many times, that was all clients really needed and wanted- someone caring to truly listen to their concerns. I never pretended to know all the answers. I may offer a few words of advice, but lastly I would listen, and help people help themselves, become their own problem-solvers.

I also told the students never to forget the value of touch. They used to say about Princess Diana, that when she touched someone, she had this incredible power and warmth about her, that many people felt a radiant feeling of kindness that went from her hand to others. I found that to be true. A simple hello, a simple act of caring went a long way. But so did touch. Not only saying hi, looking someone in their eyes, but a grasp of hands, a touch on the shoulder, that human touch which so many people lacked, missed and needed, could do so much good. It also helped people to open up, trust, and know that you were genuinely interested in them.

The final thought I mentioned was the same advice I was given back in my internship days by Eileen, my supervisor at the Manor: Always keep a sense of humor! It works, because if you mess up, in a non-emergency situation, one hundred years from now, will it matter? Always keep things in perspective, and don't be afraid to smile and laugh. When appropriate, it will make you and your clients feel better.

Keep pushing hard uphill- coast on the downhill side- and always enjoy the view at the top.

After my presentation I received a standing ovation. As the students filed out I wished them luck and asked them to keep in touch I shut off the lights in the classroom, rolling to the parking lot to catch my ride. Teaching wasn't so bad after all. I was happy I took another chance. Another experience which made me a better person.

With Liv & Barry Manilow - 1988

With singer Richard Marx - 1998

The Smith Boys
Mark, Tom, Greg, Pat, & Jim

Nephew – David; Grand-niece – Morgan; Sister - Phyllis

With Philadelphia 76ers President Pat Croce

The Best Man at Tracy and Mark's wedding
(Do I look loaded or what?!)

10. I MADE IT THROUGH THE RAIN

So, here I am. My life is a happy one. I have so much to be grateful for, so much to appreciate and so many people to thank.

Mom continues to be a fighter. She recently had both of her knees replaced-at the same time. Some people thought she was crazy. But her doctor agreed, warning her about the tough therapy that awaited her. It might take six months, maybe even an entire year until she started to feel like herself again. She wanted to get the pain over with in one dose. Plus, if she only had one knee done, she may not want to go back and have the other work done.

She came through the surgery beautifully. She only spent a few days in the hospital, then went to rehab, the same rehab hospital where I took my driver's test. She was there for two weeks, then headed home. No nursing home needed.

After more in home and outpatient therapy, she was up and walking- and even driving a car- in less then three months! Eighty-three years old, both knees replaced, and she was like herself- even better in a short time.

Her strong faith got her through. So did her determination and motivation to come home. She worried about me. Always did and always will.

I did OK during her hospital stay. After her by-pass surgery, I was more independent and knew what to expect. My family helped me when needed. And there were some tough times, I admit. But some how, some way, I would make it.

Learning to cook- and drive- are still challenges ahead of me to overcome.

My brothers and sister have grown even closer during the years. We have all learned to appreciate each other. Even though we may only see each other in one place on holidays, or at weddings or funerals, we know that we are always there for each other, no matter what. And during times in need, such as when Mom had her knees done, we bonded together for support.

My family is good to me. Now I often go to concerts or ballgames with my brothers. I have taken my sister to Manilow concerts, and she has become a fan. I learned that friends may come and go, but family is always there, during the good times and bad.

About a year ago I met an "old/new" friend. Her name is Sharon. She is a sweet, pretty, short brunette whom I had met back in the early 90s. She was a devout Manilow fan too, and we went to concerts back then, dinner, and movies. We were always strictly friends, just like Laurie and I were long ago.

Sharon was married, with two kids, which made friendship the only possibility. But that was OK. I needed a friend, and so did she.

Sharon was going through a difficult time in her marriage. She was stuck in a loveless, dependent relationship for many years. I was a friend, a good listener, and I helped her assert some independence and regain her self-respect and dignity.

She eventually got a divorce, moved into an apartment with her children, got a job and was far happier. When she met a new guy, we eventually drifted apart. She didn't have time as it was, but now with a new relationship in her life, I was a memory.

I thought of her often over the years, remembering the fun we used to have. I tried calling her one day, using her old phone number, but a woman answered, curtly answering, "There is no Sharon living here."

Oops.

I just about gave up contacting her. After all, if she wanted to keep in touch she would have. But I thought, maybe she had lost my number over the years?

Then one day a friend emailed me, and asked if the Sharon who was posting messages on the Manilow Internet web site, was the same Sharon we knew long ago?

I checked out the board. I remembered her married name. This Sharon had a different last name- but was it her maiden name? Or did she remarry?

Again with the philosophy that if you don't take a chance, you never win, I emailed her. To my pleasant surprise it was the same Sharon! She was surprised, but happy to hear from me. No, she didn't remarry. It was her maiden name.

Even better, she had recently broken up with a guy. She was free and liked it that way, but she was looking for a friend. Fate again appeared in my life.

So, we hooked up. We emailed and met again, and spent the following summer going out- movies, dinners, Manilow concerts, and day-trips down to the Jersey shore. It was nice to have someone to talk to, someone who shared common interests, and nice to have a pal again.

She remains a dear friend- and who knows what the future may hold?

I'll never forget Liv. In fact, we met again- all of us- in New York City in February of 2002. Barry was playing at Radio City Music Hall in Manhattan. I had this crazy idea. I had never seen Barry in his hometown of New York before. It started out small, and then grew. I asked Liv if she wanted to come over. She agreed, deciding to stay in New York a few days before the show. I would rent a limo to the show, and bring her back home, where she would stay for a week, before returning to Norway.

Liv always loved New York. It was still her dream to sightsee there, and aside from our brief tour during the first summer she visited, and other then traveling to and from Kennedy Airport, she still never really saw the city. So she would spend a few days in a nice hotel near Broadway, walk around the city, shop, and wait for me.

Then I decided to ask Vicki to go. She had been to Radio City before, but way back before she met me. Then I asked Sharon to go too. After her divorce she still loved Barry, but was discouraged to attend concerts by her new boyfriends. She missed the friendship of all the fans. And she missed seeing Barry in concert. So she was really happy to go along.

A black limo pulled into my driveway, and it seemed like the old days. I was a lucky guy, traveling to the Big Apple with Sharon and Vicki- along with our limo driver named Lou- traveling in style!

It was the February after September 11th, 2001. It would be a special concert, Barry's first since the World Trade Center tragedy. We expected a very emotional night. It really hit home as we approached New York. Usually the first thing we could see in the horizon from the New Jersey Turnpike would be the Twin Towers. To actually see the skyline so changed, other then on television, made us feel so sad.

We were waiting to get into the Holland Tunnel. It was rush hour and traffic was bumper to bumper. We laughed as the toll taker at the tunnel eyed the stretch limo and asked Lou, "Got anybody important in there?"

"Nah," Lou said. He heard us laugh, and apologized. "I didn't mean it that way!" he joked.

We picked up Liv at her hotel, the city so bitterly cold and windy. It was good to see her again, as always. She knew Vicki and quickly became acquainted with Sharon. We were off to Radio City, only a few blocks away.

We took some pictures in front of the theatre, and then went across the street for a bite to eat before the show. We saluted a toast- we had made it- not only to New York for the concert- but we had made it through so many years, so many ups and downs, and we were happy to be together.

The show was great. We had fantastic seats. And at the end, former President Bill Clinton made an appearance on stage to accept a check from Barry, who had donated his earnings from that night to the relief fund for the victim's families of 9/11. The total was $100,000.

We had fun on the way home, playing music and reminiscing. We would have more good times ahead.

Old friends and new friends. I was one lucky guy.

Even now, my Osteogenisis Imperfecta plays a role in my life. But I've learned to accept my condition, make the best of it, and deal with it, one day at a time. It isn't my entire life anymore, just a part of my life.

I will always have O.I. It will never go away, never be cured. But I refused to allow it to control my life. It became just another part of me, as my dimples are.

Sometimes I still dream. Not of just standing or taking a step without falling. I dream of running, something I have never done in my life. A blind person may dream of what colors would look like. Someone who is deaf may wonder what music sounds like. I dream of running, my legs long and strong, free to go wherever I want, free of the boundaries of my wheelchair. But then I always wake up. The chair is still there. My legs are still weak and disfigured. And I am left to still wonder what it is like to run, as I will forever. However, my spirit can still run, not only in my dreams, but in life itself- and beyond.

When I got a computer I had access to the Internet, so I thought I might do a little research about O.I. I especially hoped to find others out there that either had the disease or were familiar with it.

I didn't find too many support groups to contact, I guess because O.I. still remains a pretty rare disease. I read in one article where approximately one in twenty million people has the condition. I read that the life expectancy is about twenty-five years. If true, I was very lucky to be alive, beating the odds by a good twenty years. I also learned there are four different types of O.I. I'm level four, the most disabling. The methods of treatment are still about the same, using pins and rods to help strengthen and straighten the bones.

I tried not to read too much about the future and what to expect. Sometimes it is better not to know.

I saw a movie called "Unbreakable" with Bruce Willis. I was surprised and delighted to find that one of the main characters had O.I.

Any awareness about O.I. is a positive thing. There are no telethons or fundraisers for O.I. patients. So I wrote to M. Night Shyamalan, the brilliant writer/director of the movie, thanking him for including the condition in his film. I read on line that he had always been "fascinated" by the condition, and wanted to include it in a film.

The character that had O.I., played by Samuel L. Jackson, turned out to be a villain. But that was OK. Even disabled people can be "villains", like anyone else, but I hoped that people would also know that O.I. patients were not always bitter or depressed. We can be quite happy.

I was actually pleased that the character was a bad guy. Disabled people aren't always saints, nor are we always sinners. Most of us are just regular people, but often we are thought of in one extreme or the other. But I thought it was cool that Hollywood could break the stereotype and show a character with a disability that also has very passionate feelings- good or bad.

In my letter I also pointed out a few technical "flaws" in the movie. For instance, the character didn't have a tinge of blueness in the white of his eyes, a telltale sign of O.I. (many doctors in my past knew of my diagnosis just by looking into my eyes); Samuel had a perfect smile, and he wasn't four feet tall (although I guess that would have been a major special effects accomplishment).

Unfortunately, Mr. Shyamalan never wrote back. But hopefully he received my letter, especially my appreciation. I related to his movie because even though my bones were very breakable, I always felt that my spirit was "unbreakable".

I don't fracture anymore, but the stress fractures occur at times. Sometimes I don't even know when I have a crack- I've grown so used to them. New x-rays can't always reveal new fractures, because my bones have so many cracks running through them, like a road map. It's hard to tell the new from the old.

I have come to terms with my O.I. Now, I see the rest of the world as being "different". I have peace in my heart, accepting what I can't change, yet always striving to do the best I can with what I have.

I now believe there was a reason why I have O.I. Maybe I'm a better person, as well as a better social worker, because of my fate in life. Maybe having O.I. was truly a blessing in disguise.

Last winter I had pneumonia and ended up in the local emergency room. (A familiar place). The young, female doctor on call seemed more interested in my O.I. then the pneumonia.

"I've read about your condition in books," she gushed, "but I never met any one in person."

I thought she was going to ask for my autograph. That's how impressed she was. But I was used to the attention.

I've learned to appreciate life, and those you love. . Little things now make me happy, like a new wheel chair every so often. Maybe I've discovered what is really important in life. I still don't have all the answers, and maybe never will. I'm not done learning that's for sure.

Writing my story has convinced me that I wouldn't change much in my life. I look at my legs and history flashes before my eyes. If I changed anything, I may not be the guy I am today.

Through the good times and bad, I feel very lucky to have survived. And it is only the beginning.

The End.